Foreword

Deep Veils is an elegant and intelligent book on one of the most essential and controversial subjects in architecture: enclosure, walls, facades. Ever since the times of Semper, Loos and Le Corbusier, to only name three of many architects that have written on the subject, the enclosure of a building has fascinated the profession of the architect.

Especially in the past twenty years, architecture as a necessary play of space, material and weight in relation to socio-economic and political debates of our time has been under siege.

Erik L'Heureux's book on the "space of the skin" explains through a variety of very beautiful projects, and in a very readable and coherent way, the profound interrogation that every architect has when it comes to "designing the façade". The façade is also a contested term as after the modern movement it was liberated of its bearing function.

In his book, L'Heureux guides the reader through a sublime cross section of ideas on the veil, surface, enclosure, protection and many other architectural moments as one comes across a building.

If the assumption that the Façade or the outer visible layer of buildings has become the only space where the architect is free to exercise his or her authority, then with the work in this book L'Heureux proves that architecture is still very much about thickness and space, material and weight, as well as being desirable and necessary. *Deep Veils* avails.

Professor Nasrine Seraji - AA Dipl RIBA
Dean
École Nationale Supérieure d'Architecture (ENSA)
Paris - Malaquais

Deep Veils

"The building envelope is possibly the oldest and most primitive architectural element. It materializes the separation of the inside and outside, natural and artificial and it demarcates private property and land ownership (one of the most primitive political acts). When it becomes a façade, the envelope operates also as a representational device in addition to its crucial environmental and territorial roles. The building envelope forms the border, the frontier, the edge, the enclosure and the joint: it is loaded with political content... The envelope is the surface and its attachments."
– *Alejandro Zaera Polo,* The Politics of the Envelope,
A Political Critique of Materialism[1]

The Analogy of the Veil

Writing about one's own design work is one of the most difficult practices for an architect. This is because architects use drawings, models, spaces, and materials as our primary means of engagement, while verbal and written language comes second. Only after a drawing is made can it be described in language, which is how words gain currency in architecture. Words help to clarify, articulate, and reposition ideas imbedded in the act of designing — from lines to words, from words to building, from building to architecture. The following text is one such clarification of the design works I have completed over the past five years[2]. It is for me to take stock of the works and to refine the ideas behind them so that the larger theoretical ambition comes into focus.

In the following pages are ten design projects completed between 2007 and 2012 which explore various architectural ideas under the rubric of "deep veils" — a loose but convenient analogy for my current architectural preoccupations. Each project responds to questions on envelope, surface, skin, form, atmosphere, perception, as well as tropicality, and they define in various ways how a deep veil in architecture may be manifest. In simple terms, a deep veil is a screen transformed into a thickened spatial envelope and enclosure that merges optical, sensorial, and the atmospheric qualities through interference and frustration. Interference refers to a kind of perceptual haze which prioritizes obfuscation, or what Marcel Duchamp terms "delay", in the visual and atmospheric field.[3] Frustration is produced out of this delay, making the inhabitant consciously aware of architecture and their immediate world. The tension produced out of the interference created within architecture is what I am interested in.

The idea of a deep veil is a counterpoint to the much ingrained transparent and spectacular qualities of glass that perpetuate much of orthodox Modern architecture.[4] I am interested in the spatial and physical qualities of veils that are primarily composed of opaque materials which produce visual and atmospheric permeability when perforated, layered, extruded, woven, stretched, and stacked at the architectural scale. The intent of the deep veil is then to destabilize normative ideas of enclosure and reconfigure our relationship with the tropical environment into one that is more porous and integrated. Such an architecture wrestles between categories; it oscillates between the open and the closed, the exterior and the interior, walls and windows, elevations and screens, surfaces and depths, as well as presence and disappearance. With an architecture that exists between categories, our relationship to vision, space, and atmosphere opens up to produce an expanded range of experiences that are more sensorial, pleasurable, and ultimately emboldened with meaning.

Gottfried Semper in his *Style in the Technical and Tectonic Arts; or, Practical Aesthetics* (1860) correlates the history of architecture and enclosure with the long traditions of textiles and cladding: "The need for protection, cover, and spatial enclosure supplied some of the earliest inspiration for industrial invention… The use of these covers is thus older than language. As such, they form perhaps the most important element in the symbolism of architecture."[5] Adolf Loos similarly posits in *The Principle of Cladding* (1898) the lineages of architecture found in textiles: "In the beginning we sought to clad ourselves, to protect ourselves from the elements, to keep ourselves safe and warm while sleeping. We sought to cover ourselves. Originally consisting of animal furs or textiles, this covering is the earliest architectural feature."[6] The analogy between textiles and architecture is not a superficial one for textiles are woven, composed of threads of varying densities to warm and cool, protect and reveal, as well as frustrate and seduce. Veils, as an extension of these textile underpinnings, are immanently architectural and important for a robust theory of design in the tropics — not to keep ourselves warm but to modulate ourselves from heat, to ventilate our bodies, to produce hospitable spaces, and to craft and calibrate the view, light, and shadow. The deep veils referenced in these ten projects are particularly relevant in the hot and humid atmosphere of urban Singapore, where the majority of projects are built.[7] But more importantly, they seek to resurrect the (non-glass) envelope as an element that accomplishes a multitude of architectural roles, to recall its historical significance in the architectural discourse on "enclosure", "surface", and "meaning", as well as to reconsider its importance in the increasingly dense and urbanized environment of the tropics today.

Conceptual and historical foundations are at the core of my foreword. With each building and interior architectural presented, along with their respective program, structure, and type, I focus on the inherent ideological underpinnings. I am not claiming objectivity as I follow various threads of architecture and art from Semper forward, extending certain arguments and omitting others. This essay, along with the subsequent interview, traces these larger theoretical ambitions and historical influences which in tandem impact the body of my work. The project descriptions, analytical drawings, and photographs elucidate the particularities of each project and are complementary to the text;

together the merging of drawings, photographs, models, and words create a greater architectural framework. It has been an enormous undertaking over five years, forever changing my perceptions of intuition and ingenuity, surface and depth, facades and architecture.

Veils and Masks

The word "veil" comes from a late 14th century Latin word "velare", which means to cover or to enclose. Figuratively, it conveys a sense of concealment, but it is not an opaque shroud. Instead, to veil is to visually obscure so as to produce a sense of desire, as evinced in Jean Starobinski's text, *The Living Eye*, where he states, "The hidden fascinates... The fascination emanates from a real presence that obliges us to prefer what it hides, to prefer something remote, which it prevents us from attaining even as it offers itself."[8]

When we think of the hidden, we might also think of the word "mask". The term came slightly later than "veil" in the 1530s, and a mask differs from the veil in two distinct ways.

First, the mask is opaque while the veil allows visual access, though a limited one. The mask and the face behind are spatially aligned though materially distinct.[9] The mask covers and guards the face with a layer of opacity — often operating as a protective covering. This cover

transforms the face by providing an image that replaces the original with a new identity.

Second, the mask has its own structure and independent support. It maintains its form, shape, and geometry that are distinct from the face behind; indeed, the mask is its own figure. Pablo Picasso deploys the mask in the painting

1. Picasso, *Les Demoiselles d'Avignon*, 1907. The masks replace the face of the figures on the right entirely.

Les Demoiselles d'Avignon (1907), transforming the two figures on the right into entirely new constructs: clearly women but desexualized through their covering in aboriginal imagery, thus giving them a stronger presence within the composition due to their unfamiliarity and implied savagery (Figure 1).

The mask — by its production of the unfamiliar — is coupled with sinister undertones. The Medieval Latin term "masca" means a specter or nightmare. Throughout literature, the masked face has been associated not only with a new temporary identity, but one that allows for illicit and untruthful action. Both in William Shakespeare's use of masks on the characters Viola and Feste in his *Twelfth Night; or, What You Will* (1601) and also in Edgar Allan Poe's *The Mask of the Red Death* (1842), the mask was utilized as a symbol not only for empowerment but also for insidious deceit and violence.

Masks in architecture are closely aligned with façades, especially in temperate environments, where they not only cover and conceal the insides of an architectural work, but also separate the interior and exterior environments into discrete definable categories. Much of orthodox Modern architecture is predicated on "unmasking" or uncovering what is behind the façade to produce visual access into the architectural body. Thus, utilizing glass as a literal and figurative device emerges out of this context.

The veil, however, is something altogether different from the mask (or its reverse — the transparent glass-like skin). Through its visual porosity, it implies seduction and frustration over deceit, desire over the sinister, and curiosity over the abhorrent. The veil also hides, not through opacity but rather through permeability — merging the exterior surface with the interior body. The veil then oscillates between the space of honesty and visual deceit. This indeterminacy of function and meaning is what fascinates. The veil lies in a relationship with the body, requiring its structure to keep its shape while covering and protecting it. The veil is typically soft and translucent, while the mask is hard and opaque. The veil and the face become a new cohesive image, creating a new identity that requires both the face and the veil to be present. The ambiguity produced between the veil and the face — of hazy definitions and imprecise categories — is what I believe to be productive for more complex relationships between architecture, environment, and its inhabitants.

Terence Riley noted in *Light Construction* that the distinction between "transparency" and "distanced perception", or translucency, lies in architecture.[10] A distanced perception between the viewer and object through the "use of the architectural façade as a *veiling* membrane" creates a tension which heightens desire while simultaneously thwarting it. Such a membrane conceived as a veil is not merely a façade we would associate with masks, but it takes on more performative and experimental aspects between the surface and space, at once defining an envelope, yet hinting at more robust spatial configurations between the categories of interior and exterior. A deep veil is then a spatial and material concept for modulating climate, view, structure, and experience through layered and thickened surfaces, and not simply a translucent skin, surface, or free facade.

Veils in Art

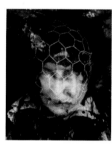

2. Gertrud Arndt, *Mask Portrait No. 16,* 1930, Dessau, Germany.

Veils as producers of indeterminacy and ambiguity are found throughout history. One such example was Gertrud Arndt (1903–2000), a pioneering textile specialist and photographer at the Bauhaus, who originally planned on being an architect. She utilized veils to reconfigure images of her face, allowing new visuals to be formed between her normative identity and her veil. In doing so, she modulated meaning and identity, as well as image and sexuality. What is critical in Arndt's deployment of the veil is that the face is interrupted, but ever visible. Facial expressions, hairstyles, and various gazes operate with the veil to reconfigure her face. In her photograph *Mask Portrait No. 16,* we can access her face through two scales of netting: a large hexagon pattern and a secondary finer-grained pattern infill (Figure 2).

Combined with her double exposure photographic techniques, the image of the face behind the veil is squeezed, flattened, and idealized into a more perfect shape. Her facial features are wrapped over and protected, yet identifiable. Likewise, in her self-portrait *Mask Portrait No. 13*, the veil covers only the lower sections of the face, creating confusion between fabric and skin, dot or facial feature, and symbol or structure (Figure 3).

3. Gertrud Arndt, *Mask Portrait No. 13*, 1930, Dessau, Germany.

Perhaps *Veil Portrait No. 13* is a more apt title as the ambiguity produced by her double reading — between an authentic image and her reconstruction — speaks of the potential of the veil as a means to destabilize our relationship with the body, and by extension, with architecture. By intervening between the body and the viewer, the veil produces a space of heightened intensity through delay, creating desire and frustration as well as admittance and denial. The delay in this example does not rely on glass; rather it is produced through a fine arrangement of opaque threads that in totality produces the distanced perception.

Similar to the work of Arndt, Optical Art explored interference within the visual field through oscillations and movements, and destabilization of visual experience through paintings and sculptures. The experiments, which coalesced into the 1965 exhibition at the Museum of Modern Art (MoMA), inform the projects represented in this

4. Julio Le Parc, *Lunettes pour une autre vision* (Glasses for another vision), 1965.

book as much as the textile attributes of the veil has. Julio Le Parc's *Lunettes pour une autre vision* (Glasses for another vision) (1965) uses "various forms of displacement, distortion, diffraction, and fragmentation to alter the entire world about them" — a prosthetic-like eyeglass that changes one's relationship to looking itself (Figure 4).

5. Julio Le Parc,
Instabilite, 1959.

6. Bridget Riley,
Current, 1964.
It was used for the
catalogue cover
of *The Responsive Eye*
at MoMA.

7. Bridget Riley,
Fall, 1963.

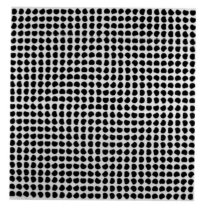

5

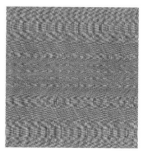

6

7

8

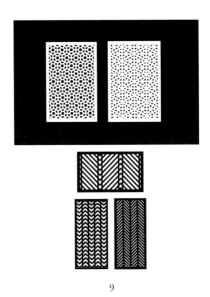

9

8. *Jali* walls from the 16th century found in India's Jehangir Mahal.

9. Top: Shaoxing, Zhejiang, 1850 (left) and Wen Shu Yuan, Chengdu, 1825 (right). Bottom three: Chengdu, 1875.

10. Chinese roof tile screen in Beijing, 2013.

10

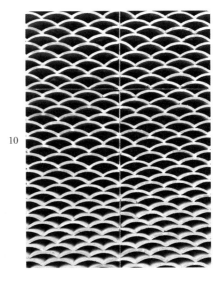

His *Instabilite* from 1959 utilizes a chamfered circle repeated throughout the visual field to produce an unsettling optical effect (Figure 5). Each circle is rotated to produce larger figures, hovering between circle and square, as well as point and wave. Likewise, Bridget Riley's *Current* from 1964 and the MoMA exhibition catalogue cover utilizes an array of thin and thick lines continuously moving in a sinous wave to capture movement within a stationary plane (Figure 6). The simple deployment of a line, albeit curved and carefully displaced from the next line, produces a visual experience oscillating between single and total, as well as static and movement. Her painting *Fall* (1963) utilizes a similar artistic device, yet stretches out the curve as though it is being pulled at one edge, anamorphically distorting the visual field (Figure 7). The fluctuating quality which we find in the works of Le Parc and Riley suggests an architectural pattern-making of veils that not only interferes with one's visual perception but also upsets commonly held notions of composition, scale, and experience itself.

Indeed, Optical Art takes on specific effects, that when deployed to architecture reasserts the temporal and visual phenomena possible within the experience of space. Optical Art provides strategies for creating new relationships between the singular piece and the whole. The field oscillates between figure and ground, as well as stasis and movement. When applied to architecture, the veil is a dynamic visual field which prevents immediate and singular readings. In the paintings of Le Parc and Riley, we see at once the modularity of the construction, the overall field, and the new figure within. But more importantly, the configuration produces a dynamic visual and tectonic quality, as though the components are stretching, swaying, and moving together. The ambiguity and contradictory elements of parts and whole, open and closed, singular and multiple, simple and complex take on both a reductive and expansive quality simultaneously. As a conceptual ambition transformed into architecture, such practice accords architecture with a deeper meaning by raising questions about use, typology, and hierarchy, and proffering multiple interpretations in place of the one, all at the same time.

The surface in Optical Art, for example, serves not as a complete barrier, but as a dynamic canvas that mediates between various layers and interpretations. The wavering visual qualities produced by the works of Le Parc and Riley suggests ways to produce material and structural systems in architecture that oscillates, vacillates, and operates in the space of ambiguity.

Veils in Architecture

There are lineages of veils not only in art but directly in the histories of architecture. Screens, ventilations blocks, breeze blocks, *jali* walls, trellises, and *brise soleils* are veils, albeit simplistic and static. Legacies of such architectural devices extend back into history from the intricately carved stone *jali*, to the carved wooden latticework of the *Mashrabiya* or *Shanasheel*, and the delicately constructed Chinese, Korean and Japanese sliding screens (Figures 8, 9 & 10). In mid 20th century modern architecture, the ventilation screen is also found in the hot and humid climate regions that span from the southern latitudes of the American continent to the tropical belts in Brazil, India, Africa, and Asia.

11. Edward Durell Stone, *US Embassy Chancery and Staff Housing,* 1955, New Delhi, India.

The architect Edward Durell Stone and designer Erwin Hauer championed such research, and both Americans deployed repeatable concrete elements to produce perforated screens across the surface in a delicate way. For example, Stone's United States embassy (1955) in New Delhi, India, utilizes the breeze block as the primary elevation component (Figure 11). Situated far beyond a large roof overhang and slender columns, the breeze block assembly unifies the elevation. The blocks, in this case, dissolve into an architecturally scaled surface of grand proportions appropriate to the climatic context of India. Since the demands of industrial casting favored repeatability, the deployment of

12. Erwin Hauer, *Design 5*, 1956, Miami, Florida, USA. Interior for the First National Bank of Miami.

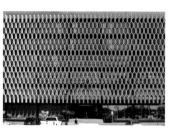

13. Vladimir Ossipoff, *IBM Building*, 1962, Honolulu, Hawaii, USA.

Stone's ventilation blocks were limited to stacking of the singular module.

Erwin Hauer's more sculptural and graphic screens attempt to dissolve the discrete repeatable element into a larger tessellated pattern, merging individual units into a unified surface (Figure 12). Primarily limited to interior applications, Hauer sought to spatialize the single screen with a thickened depth by deploying more complex spatially-derived units that produced overlaps, layers, and complexity in both two and three dimensions. His work begins to combine the static quality of modular construction with the visual dynamism suggested by Optical Art, and it is no coincidence that his influential work emerges at about the same period. Many architects from the mid 20th century worked through similar experiments: the IBM Building (1962) in Honolulu Hawaii by architect Vladimir Ossipoff, Curtis and Davis' IBM (now United Steelworkers) Building (1962), and the AXA Life Building (1975) in Singapore by James Ferrie and Partners are but a small sample of a much longer list (Figures 13, 14 & 15). Yet, all were beholden to the realities of fabrication during their time: the demand for the repeatable element.

14. Curtis and Davis, IBM (now *United Steelworkers*) Building, 1962, Pittsburgh, Pennsylvania, USA.

15. James Ferrie and Partners, *AXA Life Building*, 1975, Singapore.

The "Reveal"

The terms "veil" and "reveal" are interrelated especially when applied to architecture. Etymologically, the word "reveal" comes from the late 14-century old French word *"reveler"* or the Latin *"revelare"* (incorporating *"velare"* as in veil) meaning to "uncover, disclose". Yet, 20th century modern architecture has been a history of removing the veil so to speak, prioritizing the reveal over the veil, exposure over covering. Reveals are found in architectural discourse at the scale of the detail, where a small shadow gap is produced at the intersection of two materials. Mies van der Rohe was particularly fond of the reveal, highlighting the distinction between two materials. For example, in the Barcelona Pavilion of 1929, there was a clear reveal between the panels of the golden onyx wall surfaces. Reveals were also found at the intersection of the green alpine marble slabs along the interior pool walls of the same project. Mies' later work at the Seagram Building (1958) reveals the corner intersection of each plane of the curtain wall by articulating the joint of each elevation. These reveal joints may be seen as a critical reaction against traditional building techniques, where joints were commonly concealed and masked over with a trim element. The reveal detail exposes the material interface in the most optically evident manner possible while eliminating ornaments typically applied to trim pieces.

Glass has been the most spectacular tool of such revelation. Ludwig Hilberseimer's essay *Glasarchitektur* formulates the symbolism of glass as the physical manifestation of a truthful architecture.[11] Glass architecture was perceived not only as the reveal to the truthfulness to construction, but also as the lens to authentic culture by extension. Joseph Paxton's Crystal Palace of 1851 provided a vision of an open lightweight architecture of almost full visual transparency. The Reliance Building of 1895 by Burnham and Root utilized large swaths of plate glass to open the building to natural light while expressing the structural framework of its façade. Mies' Friedrichstrasse Skyscraper Project (1921) and his un-built glass skyscraper for Berlin (1922) employed glass curtain walls to reveal the structure and interiors of the architecture while symbolically positioning glass as a symbol of the modern. These large areas of industrially produced glass also facilitated penetration of sunlight indoors, a reflection of climatic ideas calibrated to the temperate climate where heating was prioritized over cooling demands.

Modern architecture has embraced the concept of the reveal both as a technical detail device and a larger theoretical construct manifest in glass — to expose and reveal material truths, to express honesty in the architectural body, to remove ornamentation, and to show — to reveal the interior through transparency. Loos' statement, "Be truthful, nature only sides with truth", is indicative of such a modernist underpinning, as is his view that "Each and every material has its own vocabulary of forms and no material can appropriate the forms of another".[12] Louis Kahn has a similar adage that states "Architecture is the reaching out for the truth." Amongst many other sayings from a long list of masters, these set the foundation for an architectural discourse within the modern project of "truthfulness", "honesty", and "openness". Indeed, the act of revealing both literally (in the detail) and figuratively (in the act of making architecture), has arguably become the preoccupation of architectural discourse from Louis Sullivan onwards when he states that "form ever follows function".

The equation of modernity with the ambition of honest revelation reached an early peak with the publication of *The International Style: Architecture Since 1922* by Henry-Russell Hitchcock and Philip Johnson, which recorded the *Modern Architecture: International Exhibition* at the MoMA in 1932. Hitchcock and Johnson elucidated a contemporary architecture where the celebration of technology, industrialization, glass, steel, and concrete opened up architecture to a future that was transparent and visually open, based on elemental volumes and expulsion of ornamentation. Transparency, curtain walls, and glass were equated with the tenets of "truth" and "righteousness".

In its endeavor for "International" prominence, the "Style" soon made its way to the tropics. Indeed, for many modernizing regions particularly Singapore, glass curtain-wall and air-conditioning appeared to be an enticing representation of an industrial and "modern" future. They represented an industrial transformation to an atmospheric reality where climate was conquered and nature was disciplined through technological and mechanical know-how. By subjugating the tropical environment into a temperate simulation, they acted as a proof that the region had made it into the league of "modernized" and temperate-appearing world.

In the now famous words of Singapore's first Prime Minister Mr. Lee Kuan Yew, "air-conditioning was the best invention of the twentieth century."[13] Air-conditioning, pervasively applied throughout Singapore, thrust her out of the tropics into the temperate First World both atmospherically and symbolically. Vernacular methods of ventilation and tropical typologies were replaced by sealed curtain walls and a brand new energy that was dependent on the industrial aesthetic. The ubiquitous application of modernist idioms and technology in Singapore signified that the First World had arrived too.

What was lost in the adoption of the "best invention of the twentieth century" was not just the performative and passive knowledge that emerged out of a tropical climate, but also the promise of a more robust architectural discourse between the screened architectural body, visual interference, and atmospheric transformation. Such a promise, found in much of the vernacular tradition, would modulate environment, atmosphere, and architecture in a carefully calibrated passive way by asserting the power of architecture to create a range of enjoyable spatial experiences. Indeed, a more "honest" approach to atmospheric integration was replaced, or masked over, with a preference for the technological aesthetic of glass and the artificially consistent interior climates made possible by air conditioners, regardless of the energy being consumed.[14]

We may understand Mies' Friedrichstrasse Project or his later Farnsworth House as the manifestation of modernist ideals in the twentieth century. It is an architecture based on material reveals, transparency, and openness, actualized as large sheets of glass sandwiched between sleek industrially produced planes. Visibility is immediate: one can see through the entire structure, flattening and de-materializing the enclosed space. However, by seeking to introduce enclosure and shadow, tropical materialization in architecture is an inverse operation. This is theorized as a deep veil of interference. Indeed, to veil is not to entirely conceal; rather, it is to layer degrees of interference deep within the structures such that visual perception is delayed. The effect of this delay is, as Riley notes, "a voyeuristic condition… [that] entraps our desires and attracts us by keeping us at a distance."[15]

If we posit that the mask is the site of the untruthful, the deceitful, and the ornamented that is to be eradicated from modern architecture through transparency and glass, then screened, atmospheric, and permeable —veiled architecture— defies the categorization.[16] This is because the veil is both truthful and camouflaging, both encloses and exposes, both wraps and indicates. The veil seduces and frustrates. As Hal Foster elaborates in his text *The Art-Architecture Complex* (2011), a shift has occurred from the modern machine for living to that of a postmodern machine—not a machine of symbolic architectural references but one that reveals and, more significantly for the tropics, conceals.

Tropical Emigrations

Architects did attempt to produce modern architecture calibrated to the tropical milieu via passive means, avoiding the transparent symbols of early 20th century modernism. Le Corbusier, Charles Correa, B. V. Doshi, Geoffrey Bawa, and Kahn among others produced alternative theoretical trajectories as robust counter-responses to the honest and transparent architectural adages that percolated throughout architecture for the temperate environment. By the late 1960s, such counter-

23

responses were well-articulated in the annuals of the Department of Tropical Architecture at the Architectural Association and throughout the tropical region proper. Maxwell Fry, Jane Drew, and Otto Koenigsberger, all respectively penned architectural theories based on climatic control after their return from Nigeria and India, suggesting a variety of technical and architectural solutions.[17] Yet, their architectural, structural, and

16. Le Corbusier, *Capitol Complex, The Secretariat*, 1965, Chandigarh, India.

symbolic ideas were subsumed to tropical functionality and solution-driven performance, concerned primarily with mitigation of heat and humidity. The spatial, experiential qualities of architecture were by and large left out of the conversation.

The box-like US consulate in Luanda, Angola (1961), designed by Kahn, experimented with the double envelope to mitigate the intense tropical climate. There are other somewhat less

17. Oscar Niemeyer, *Edifício Copan*, 1966, São Paulo, Brazil.

successful traces, including Corbusier's Capitol Complex (1965) and its amazingly complex *brise soleil* (though the large open plazas are problematic) (Figure 16), Oscar Niemeyer's Edifício Copan (1966) with its sinuous long curved deep façade (Figure 17), or Bawa's Kandalama Hotel in Sri Lanka (1995), which is covered in vegetation that speaks of an exterior envelope thickened through the layering of a veil-like organic membrane (Figure 18).

18. Geoffrey Bawa, *Kandalama Hotel*, 1995, Dambulla, Sri Lanka.

19. Le Corbusier, *Villa Shodan*, 1956, Ahmedabad, India.

Whether it is composed in concrete, steel, or vegetation, these thick envelopes modulated the climate and view, while screening the architectural spaces within.

Corbusier's Villa Shodan (1956), a box-like opaque volume capped by a large roof floating above the spaces, speaks not of openness or honesty, but of shadow and concealment (Figure 19). The volumetric space is wrapped in an atmosphere of darkness — the very qualitative affect that renders the villa far removed from the normative discourses of modernism that Corbusier earlier championed as "bathed in light". The Ahmedabad Textile Mill Owners' Association House (1954), also designed by Corbusier in the same city, is encircled with a deep concrete volume (Figure 20). The *brise soleil* puts the interior into the shade so as to minimize thermal gain (though somewhat less successful due to its orientation), while allowing specific views to the exterior. However, the depth of the *brise soleil's* size is so great in relation to the body that

20. Le Corbusier, *Ahmedabad Textile Mill Owners' Association House*, 1954, Ahmedabad, India.

it covers and becomes a volumetric space in itself — literally part of the architectural body. The large enclosures of the Shaheed Suhrawardy Medical College Hospital in Kahn's National Assembly Complex building (1982) in Dhaka also uses deep volumes to produce large shaded verandahs shielding the main interior spaces (Figure 21). Similarly Charles Correa's Kanchanjunga Apartments (1983) uses deep subtractions from the building volume to carve out verandah-like terraces, moving the interior spaces deep within from the perimeter envelope (Figure 22). Here, the volume is deployed as the thermal barrier, placing space into deep shadow while allowing the inhabitant the privilege of viewing onto the exterior.

Singapore and the larger region had their own vernacular strategies of atmospheric and optical control that were expressed in vernacular shop houses as well as colonial bungalows (Figure 23). Within these typologies, two tropical strategies predominated. One was the veiled verandah and the other was the courtyard. The verandah, employed by the British during their colonial occupation of Singapore, circumscribed the living quarters with a shaded portico that buffered against tropical heat. At the scale of a large room surrounding the house, the verandah when covered in trellised screens, operable rattan shades, or louvered shutters, served as a viewing deck to the landscape beyond.

21. Louis Kahn, *Shaheed Suhrawardy Medical College Hospital, National Assembly Complex*, 1982, Dhaka, Bangladesh.

The verandah could be read as a doubling or thickening of the envelope, and as a volumetric shading device that enclosed the interior private space. While mediating two environments of exterior and interior, the verandah itself becomes a third. Contrary to a building "skin" or a thin "surface" that connotes a linear demarcation between two boundary conditions, the verandah is a *volumetric veil* which *expands* the boundary situation into a spatial gradient. In addition, these verandahs are persistently found in black-and-white bungalows which are often situated in manicured lawns that buffered against tropical jungles. The lawn represented an extension of this spatial atmosphere which mediated between architecture and wild, viewed and viewer, as well as subject and object. Neither inside nor outside, the verandah

22. Charles Correa, *Kanchanjunga Apartments,* 1983, Mumbai, India.

23. Public Works Department, *Colonial Bungalow*, 1900, No. 6 Goodwood Hill, Singapore.

operated as an in-between, neither entirely public nor entirely private.

The verandahs were lifted about a meter off the ground or more, creating a gap that permitted cross breezes to cool the floor plane while preventing the warmed earth from conducting heat into the interiors. The spatial heightening of the verandah and living quarters denoted power not only of the British over their subjects through the production of hierarchy and distance, but also over Nature by separating architecture from jungle and heat from hospitality.

24. Author, *Shop House for a Photographer*, 2013, Emerald Hill, Singapore.

The second tropical strategy was the use of the internal courtyard. The shophouse courtyard in particular was built by the Chinese diaspora in Singapore as the other pole in the litany of tropical devices (Figure 24). Inward-looking and embedded within the interiority of architecture, the shophouse courtyard re-directed the outward-looking gaze into an insular perspective. The courtyard was a constructed landscape garden that formed a communal space for the inhabitants while inviting the elements deep into the interiors. The courtyard brought reflected light into the long and narrow configurations of a shophouse. As it was open to the sky and rain, the courtyard served not only to bring light and fresh air into the interior but also to vacate smells and fumes. Creating spaces of optical exchange between the different storeys with an element of disorienting vertigo, while amplifying cross-ventilation too.

Deep Veils

If the temperate — and the majority of modern architecture for that matter — is the pushing of the interior as close to the exterior envelope as possible and orientating the building to allow the sun to warm the interior, then tropical architecture is the reverse. It pulls the interior deep within, creating a depth such that shade is paramount, the sun is hidden from view, and breezes are amplified rather than blocked. What results is a deep envelope, a *deep veil* where shadow, concealment, and veiling are prioritised over transparency, revelation, and honesty. Traditionally, a large roof overhang served this purpose, dissolving the elevation into dark shadow. However, with the closer building proximities and demands of higher built densities found in Singapore and much of urbanizing Southeast Asia, the large roof overhang is no longer effective or possible. Buildings today are put in close proximity to one another and to the streets in which they face, built higher, and of more stories. In this context, the primacy of the elevation takes hold, and this displaces the horizontal plane of the roof with the vertical plane as a crucial architectural element. From the demands for intensification of interior area to the exterior climatic demands of performance, and to the experiential and symbolic attributes of the building's surface, the challenges of the vertical plane is the contested site of architecture today.

I am interested in the challenges of the vertical plane — conceived as a deep veil — as *the* entire architectural project, not simply a cladding or a decorative screening element. For such an architectural device to operate as a deep veil, I believe it should satisfy four specific criteria.

1

The interference between the envelope and the interior redefines the architecture such that a new architectural structure emerges: a deep veil that combines structure and architecture into a cohesive whole.

2

The form, pattern, and structure of the deep veil, is designed to destabilize normative architectural codes including room, storey, and type. Much like how a veil upsets facial symmetry and the visibility of facial features, an ambiguity of architectural space is created.

3

The deep veil calibrates view and light through its surface depth, porosity, and structure to empower the inhabitant with a space of thermal comfort and optical privacy.

4

Through its permeability, the deep veil modulates surrounding atmospheres passively, creating flexible spatial zones between exterior and interior spaces to produce a graduated spatial experience.

In short, a deep veil operates as interference, and by doing so it unifies architecture and structure, architecture and scale, architecture and view, as well as architecture and atmosphere.

A screen, trellis, or perforated surface may be a type of veil as is a *brise soleil*; yet, not all are deep. The word "deep" comes from the old English "deop" which means profound and mysterious, and has connotations of emerging from the ground. Both thickness and the mysterious quality are critical architectural components of the *deep*, the former being spatial and the latter being experiential.

The majority of the works presented in this book deploy a mix of these four theoretical components to produce variations of deep veils, transforming each project's relationship with structure, scale, view, pattern and atmosphere. The deep veil is not limited to façades, and it extends throughout the entire structure of the architectural body, both on its exterior and its interior, producing a cohesive architectural language that continually modulates views and atmospheres, experience and use. The veils, coupled with the tropical architectural techniques of shadow, layers, verandahs, and courtyards, enable variations in climate and experience.

There are certain predilections in this body of work. One tendency is to use deep veils as a means to wrap and cover the architecture with a cohesive material surface that acts as a thickened wrapper. The physical qualities of the wrapper's material are then amplified such that a more monolithic form springs. This is a resistance to orthodox ideas of dematerialization and literal transparency via glass found throughout Modern Architecture. Minimizing the material palette reinforces the importance of those materials selected while assisting in amplifying the singular — though not simplistic — configuration. Monolithic forms tend towards the platonic, yet they are slightly skewed or mutated in plan or section, and sometimes both. This occurs as a result of the elemental geometry colliding with site or program specifics. The collision produces tension between the two states of ideal and context, and is subsequently made manifest in the architecture. Windows, punctures for aperture, and "frames" are purposefully repressed for the preference towards the totalizing surface, screen, and veil. By doing so, the architectural surfaces are unified and made more apparent visually. The veiled surface modulates the effects of atmosphere in a graduated way. The resulting effects of light and shadow produce internal spaces of sanctity, privacy, and quiet, which are important qualities in an increasingly urbanized tropical environment. My explorations yield a preference for specific architectural tropes including courtyards, skylights, and stretched trapezoidal forms in section. By looking up into these large vertical spaces, both exterior and interior, a sense of grandeur and delight is produced while the spaces also serve to circulate and ventilate air and heat. When light is filtered from above, it produces a gravitational center to the plans without relying on the normative conventions of symmetry.

Each of the projects can be placed into two basic categories. One expression is as a thickened surrounding envelope on the outside of the building, either in plan or section, that has a direct impact on exterior configuration and the interior space. This is predominantly found in urban-sized projects, including *A Stereoscopic House, Pile Houses, Hut House, Pop-Up, Venice Biennale, Prototype House, Neighborhood Towers,* and *A Simple Factory Building.* The second category is defined by interior scales which utilize similar architectural devices, yet are calibrated to a more experiential and visual realm, as seen in *Container/Canopy, Deep Envelopes,* and *A Simple Interior.* As smaller scaled architectures, the interior projects offer sites of investigation that often inform the larger scaled architectural work as they allowed ideas on the veil to be tested with expediency.

For example, there are parallels between *A Simple Factory Building* and *A Simple Interior* where gradation of porosities produce unsettling visual fields recalling the optical effects created by Le Parc and Riley discussed of earlier. The ladder is wrapped in a continuous surface of gradient veil that shrinks and swells in scale, directing the eye throughout its length. *A Simple Interior,* through a subtle displacement of the brick coursing and adjustments in the stacking dimension in plan, creates a dynamic visual field moving across the horizon. This field filters views to the exterior while destabilizing notions of the straight and even elevation. The two projects are of vastly different scales, yet they share important commonalities. The Exterior Insulation Finishing System (EIFS) pattern for *A Simple Factory Building* is calibrated to a distant view where the vantage point is from both the exterior and the interior where one looks through the deep veil. The brick pattern of *A Simple Interior* is scaled for a closer proximity between the body of the viewer and the screen itself, allowing the senses to engage the material and construction methodology of the wall as much as looking through it.

Another two examples are *A Stereoscopic House* and the interior of *Container/Canopy.* In the former, various view trajectories are layered with perforated screens, sliding doors, translucent channel glass, and herringbone thermal wrappers that create a multitude of viewing possibilities as one moves through and about the house. There is a spatial division between two interior solids on the upper levels, which is

25. Luigi Moretti, *Palazzina Il Girasole*, 1950.

bisected by an exterior void. Recalling Luigi Moretti's *Casa Il Girasole* (1950), the exterior space is pulled to the centre of the house to create a large four-storey courtyard (Figure 25). The surface of the façade is then pulled deep within the building, creating a large verandah with two bedrooms facing each other. In this juxtaposition, inside and outside, private and public, as well as closed and open categories are put into an ambiguous relationship. Overhangs, screens, and reflections on transparent and translucent glass produce a kaleidoscopic effect where views and atmospheres are mixed together in a dynamic spatial experience. The envelope is composed of a timber thermal and rain screen patterned in a herringbone configuration that mitigates solar load while unifying the exterior surface of the house by merging ceiling, elevation, and roof into one cohesive system.

The *Container/Canopy* project utilizes similar architectural devices for completely different ends. A large box-like volume also in herringbone timber is purposely opaque and provides limited views into the interior. The timber cladding unifies the space, merging interior and exterior as well as wall and floor surfaces into a single design. Inside, the three suspended volumes loosely define a centre living room-like space. Each volume also serves as a dressing room, which is raised slightly above the floor. In a nod to Duchamp's *Étant donnés* (1966), each room is punctuated by a peep hole hanging rod, allowing the exchange of views between the two categories of the private and the public. Less screen-like, *Container/Canopy* uses sight lines, reflections, volumetric position, as well as depth to create spatial and optical experiences consistent with ideas embedded in the other projects.

But there are finer degrees of differences that elucidate the analogy of the deep veil in architectural terms. These are:

Thick veils (Figure 26)

The thick veil is one with extrusion and depth within the veil's material itself. It is a three dimensional surface. By being thick, it is wall-like, has mass, substance, and weight. Depending on the thickness and perforation, the thick veil can be read in various ways. For example, a thick veil can be opaque when viewed obliquely, or look transparent when seen from the front. *A Simple Factory Building*, *Neighborhood Towers*, *Hut House*, and *Venice Biennale* explore this changing relationship.

Layered veils (Figure 27)

The layered veil is typically thin, two dimensional, and lightweight. Because of its thinness, such a veil is often cut out of a singular material such as aluminum or fabricated of timber. By layering the thin veils in space, one onto another, not only is interference produced between two sides of a single veil, but a dynamic quality is also created from the interaction and interference of multiple layers. *A Stereoscopic House*, *A Simple Interior* and *Pile Houses* are such examples.

Cohesive veils (Figure 28)

The cohesive veil dissolves the individual constituent components of the veil into a larger surface. Through material consistency or control of the visual proximity to the veil itself, the skin-like and surface quality of the aggregation is reinforced. Variations in the module complement this totality such that consistent repetition is avoided in preference for the field over the stacked, the surface over the component. *A Simple Factory Building*, *Neighborhood Towers*, *Hut House*, and *A Simple Interior* use variations of the surface aggregation to produce new dynamic field-like qualities.

Spatial veils (Figure 29)

The spatial veil takes on qualities of being thick, layered, and cohesive, though its fundamental attribute is to deploy space within and between veils so that we experience the spatial veil physically, not just visually.

Verandahs, double envelopes, wrapped terraces, breezeways, and thick casework are such spaces and these qualities are found in *A Simple Factory Building, Neighborhood Towers, A Simple Interior, A Stereoscopic House, Pile Houses, Venice Biennale,* and *Pop-Up.*

These examples extend the architectural analogy of the deep veil, suggesting that the surface has the capacity to be modeled in such a way to create a dialogue and dynamic tension between volume and flatness. *Pile Houses* deploy comparable volumetric subtractions and additions, as found in *A Stereoscopic House,* by subtracting volumes and verandah-like spaces from the main architectural body, while pressing and extending other areas about the elevation and section to strategically let in light and accommodate cross ventilation.

Likewise, *A Simple Factory Building, Neighborhood Towers, Venice Biennale, Hut House, A Simple Interior,* and *Deep Envelopes* all deploy deep envelopes as thickened surfaces to modulate climate, view, and optical relationships. In *A Simple Factory Building,* a thick 1,200 millimeters deep envelope composed of lightweight EIFS Dryvit, produces a thick layering of visual and atmospheric control by utilizing material innovations and digital fabrication to produce a lightweight dynamic veil. This depth presents opportunities to experiment with porosity and visibility, shadow and breeze; and yet depth does not visually need to equate to heaviness. The veil is four times lighter than the equivalent configuration in concrete. *Neighborhood Towers* extends this envelop strategy to perform as the primary structural system too, carrying structural loads throughout the project. In this example, the structural load of the building is carried by the deep veil finely distributed about its exterior.

Indeed, new digital fabrication and simulation technologies are critical to the production of the various types of the deep veil today which are both efficient in weight and cost while enabling the dynamic configurations to be realized. By doing so, it enables the architectural veil to become a more vibrant surface with depth as it expands the

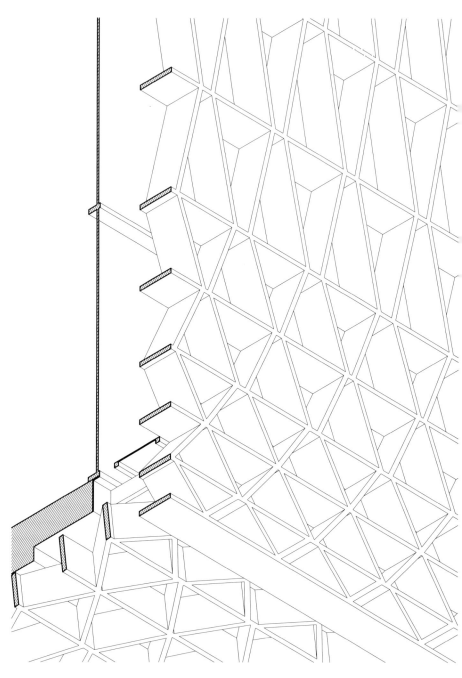

26. Thick veils

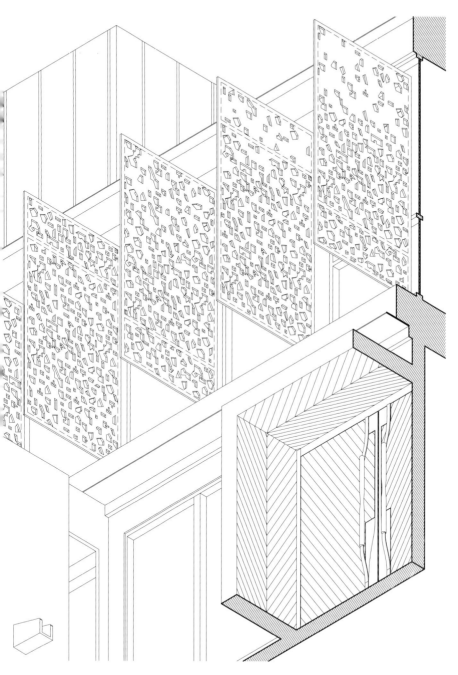

7. Layered veils

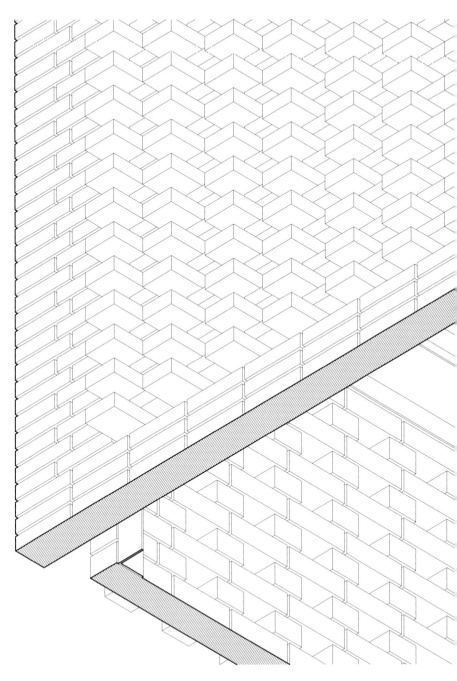

28. Cohesive veils

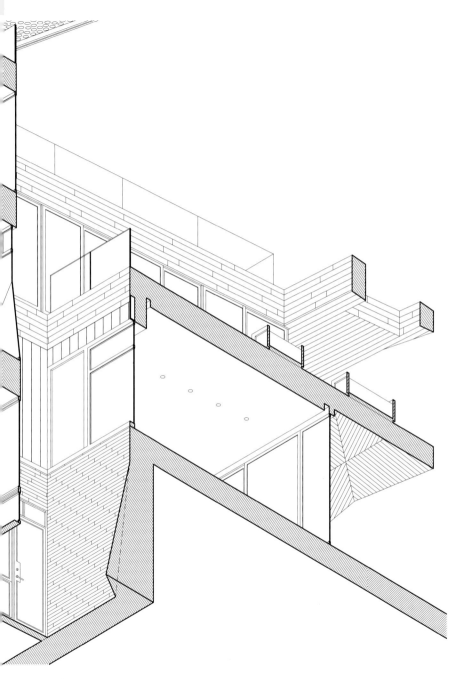

29. Spatial veils

possibilities of the deep veil beyond simple static screens and discrete repeatable elements. By utilizing advanced 3D-modeling software, digital fabrication, CNC cutting, and lightweight materials, new patterns and expressions of the deep veil are possible far beyond the repeated elements from mid 20th century modernism. By allowing for small changes within the module, a dynamic optical and experiential quality is produced by modulating light, view, and atmosphere in a more complex and intricate manner. This is a direct response to the climate. Producing variations and dynamics of light and shadow through the deep veil is necessary to overcome the atmospheric banality of Southeast Asia's uniform sun path and intensity, seasonal sameness, and the ubiquity of the overcast day.

At the same time, the materials deployed oscillate between the rough and the refined, as well as the handcrafted and the technologically precise. Rough cast concrete is coupled with new forms of plaster-coated expanded styrene that are cut by computer-controlled routers. Aged timber spread in a traditional herringbone pattern is deployed in a novel application by wrapping the entire surface of the house. Brick is coursed with subtle undulations that create dynamic optical screens which are fabricated with the assistance of digital simulations and machine-cut templates. Skylights bring light into interior spaces from above, yet they are screened with laser-cut panels. By doing so, the architecture combines regional, contextual, and contemporary elements. Often, these explorations result in heightened tactility of the architectural surface and reaffirm the textile underpinnings of the projects in general.

The deep veil modulates and often mitigates the energy dependence that air conditioning brings, an important consideration in the long-term consumption pattern of any building. Passive atmospheres are encouraged wherever possible, while discrete areas have the option for air conditioning; offering a choice rather than a necessity.

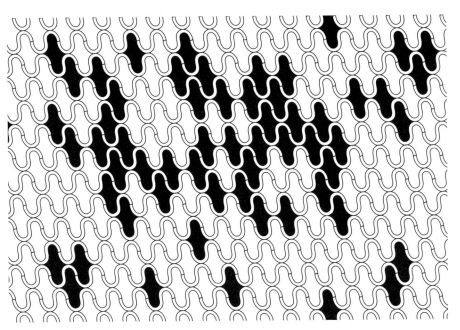

30. Lunar New Year "S" Pattern

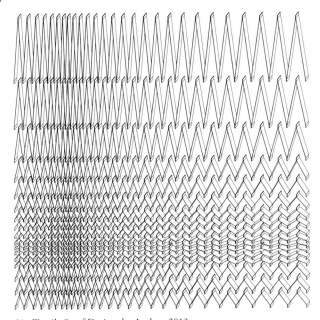

31. Textile Scarf Design, by Author, 2013

Urban Implications

The materialization of deep veils, as they have been envisioned in the work, also possesses important urban strategies. One is based on the implicit understanding that deep veils are not conceived of as solid surfaces, but are aggregates of smaller fine-grained or minutely woven elements that produce a whole. When these elements are rendered at an architectural scale, it begins to take on an urban aggregative quality. The combination of these smaller scaled elements and building forms becomes a means of creating indoor and outdoor spaces that are porous to the exterior atmosphere. Views between the multitudes of volumes are exchanged, calibrated, and interrupted based on position and orientation. Thus, the interior and exterior environments operate on a

continuum of atmospheres where heat is expelled, light is modulated, and breezes circulated. In this field of collections, the conventional definitions of interior, exterior, figure, and ground are brought into an ambiguous relationship, and in so doing, amplify and encourage pedestrian-scaled inhabitation,

32. A model of *Neighborhood Towers.*

neighborliness, and a general sense of community. The urban scale of the *Pile Houses, Neighborhood Towers* and *Prototype House/Neighborhood* suggests the potential for such aggregative spatial making (Figures 31 & 32). Small-scaled volumes positioned in tight proximity to one another create a thick blanket of urban pedestrian-scaled qualities. In *Neighborhood Towers*, the alleyways and passageways intermingle about the collection of buildings that merge at various levels to produce larger floor plates, upsetting our understanding of figure and ground as well as field and object. Wrapped in a similar language of *trellis*-like deep veils, a cohesive and coherent language brings the blocks into dialogue with one another, while serving as the primary structural system. The tight alleyway not only recalls the traditional urban form of the historical areas of the city in which the project exists, it also directly encourages pedestrian-scaled public inhabitation. By aggregating smaller elements across the urban field, a closer relationship between interior and exterior, private and public spaces, individual and neighborhood, as well as architectural and the natural world are made possible. The resulting architectural forms are neither fully open nor completely honest as orthodox Modernism expects; rather the smaller fine grained elements produce a modulation between the individual and the collective and also difference and coherence. My hope is that such strategies will inform the work as it takes on greater scale and public engagement.

This collection of words, drawings, and photographs are synthesized into a coherent thought process on architecture in the tropics, atmosphere, and what has become a long standing preoccupation with deep veils. Most importantly, this book reflects and formulates the relevance of such ambitions and the resulting meanings. Transformed from the robust architectural and artistic productions of the 1950s and 1960s and traced from the historiographies of Semper and Loos, the work here reaffirms the promise of architecture not to dissolve, but to amplify its presence such that it can impact experience, atmosphere, and our built world in a more delightful and integrated manner. Architecture is the production of experience built from drawings and ideas made into space and material. Many of the ideas shown in the following drawings and photographs do not make it into words written here. Jacques Herzog once noted, "Architecture is Architecture, Literature is literature…and a building is a building. It cannot be read like a book; it doesn't have any credits, subtitles, or labels like pictures in a gallery".[18] The intent of this book is to clarify and thus reframe some of the implicit thoughts in the work and to anticipate the direction of future works in the next five years. In this sense, it is at once reflective and a projection.

Returning to Semper, he states that "The essence of architecture is its covering layer rather than its material structure. The cover's purpose is the opposite of that of the binding. Everything closed, protected, enclosed, enveloped, and covered presents itself as a *unified* surface, as a

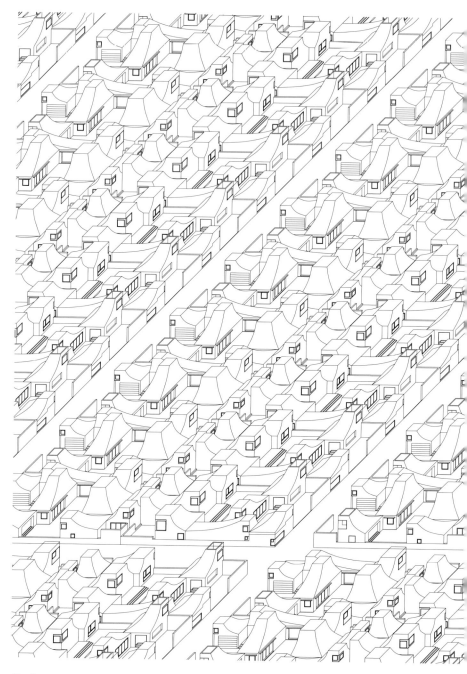

33. Prototype House/Neighborhood

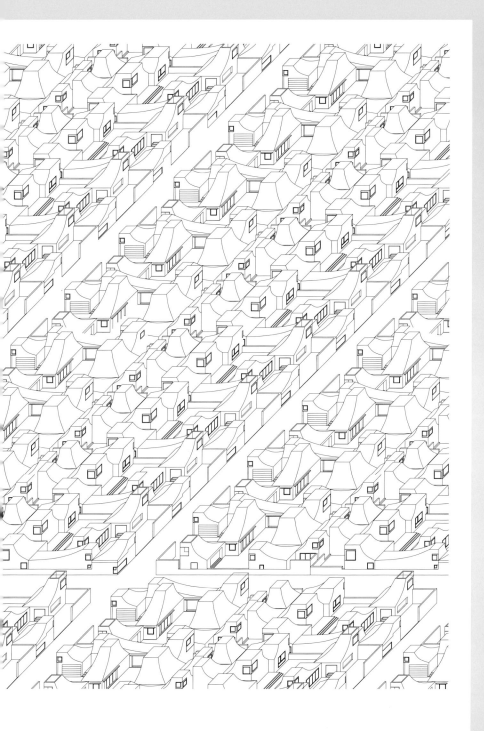

collective…"[19] My understanding of the veil has gone from a surface as a wrapper initially to an architecture that is more unified spatially and structurally — a unification of the covering and the binding. Furthering my investigations into deep veils, my next step is to focus on the integration of natural and organic materials to surface and structure and to deepen architecture and its relationship to the environment. This is the promise of the analogy of the deep veil: that it takes on more and more roles. In each project, the deep veils become the crux of the architecture instead of being regarded merely as facades, decorations, or functional cladding.

Reduction requires amplitude. To reduce the architecture to a veil means that it has to do a lot more work. The more essentialized the architecture becomes, the more unified it is; the more it needs to do, then the more depth it acquires.

Bibliography

Foster, Hal. *The Art-Architecture Complex.* London: Verso, 2011.

Hilberseimer, Ludwig. "Glasarchitektur." In *Die Form 4.19* (1929): 521-522.

Kipnis, Jeffrey, and Todd Gannon. *The Light Construction Reader.* New York: The Monacelli Press, 2002.

Loos, Adolf. "The Principle of Cladding." In *On Architecture*, translated by Michael Mitchell, 42-46.

Riley, Bridget. *Bridget Riley: Complete Prints 1962-2010.* London: Ridinghouse, 2012.

Riley, Terence. *Light Construction.* New York: The Museum of Modern Art, 2004.

Rowe, Colin, and Robert Slutzky. "Transparency: Literal and Phenomenal." *Perspecta 8* (1963): 45-54.

Semper, Gottfried. *Style in the Technical and Tectonic Arts; or, Practical Aesthetics.* Santa Monica, California: Getty Trust Publications, 2004.

Starobinski, Jean. *The Living Eye.* Cambridge, Massachusetts: Harvard University Press, 1989

Notes

1   Zaera-Polo, Alejandro. "The Politics of the Envelope" in *Log* 13/14 (Fall 2008): 193-207.

2   Five years is a short time frame and the collection and scale of the projects are small, but I believe the ideas are applicable to larger and more complex scales of architecture.

3   Marcel Duchamp describes in his notes on *The Bride Stripped Bare by Her Bachelors, Even (The Large Glass)* as a "delay in glass", referring to the suggested tension produced between the Bride on the upper panel and the nine bachelors on the lower panel. These notes were published in 1934 as part of the 94 items that made up *The Green Box.*

4   See the 1994 *Light Construction* exhibition at the Museum of Modern Art, New York, and *The Light Construction Reader* where various architects and theorists describe glass as a veil. Note that there is a specific concentration on glass, and glass-looking (ice) elements, at the expense of other material manifestations of the veil analogy.

5   Semper, Gottfried. *Style in the Technical and Tectonic Arts; or, Practical Aesthetics*, 1860, 123.

6   Loos, Adolf. "The Principle of Cladding." In *On Architecture*. California: Ariadne Press, 2002.

7   The October 1969 issue of *Rumah: Journal of the Singapore Institute of Architects* juxtaposed photographs of architecture with various textiles and prints. Though the juxtaposition was not extrapolated in words, the association between architecture and textiles was clearly evident in the collection.

8   Starobinski, Jean. *The Living Eye.* Cambridge: Harvard University Press, 1989, 1-2. Terence Riley also quotes from this text in his 1994 introduction to the *Light Construction* exhibition at the Museum of Modern Art, New York.

9   The face is conveniently used for the reader to visualise. We might easily replace the term "face" with "architecture" to more closely align the metaphor with the contents of the book.

10 Riley, Terence. *Light Construction*, The Museum of Modern Art, New York, 1994.

11 Hilberseimer, Ludwig. "Glasarchitektur." In *Die Form* 4.19, 1929.

12 Loos, "The Principles of Cladding", 42.

13 "Success Stories: Lee Kuan Yew." Singapore: Innoform Media Pte Ltd, 2001. See http://snb.nl.sg/det_12906014.aspx "Air conditioning was a most important invention for us (Singapore), perhaps one of the signal inventions of history. It changed the nature of civilization by making development possible in the tropics. Without air conditioning you can work only in the cool early-morning hours or at dusk. The first thing I did upon becoming prime minister was to install air conditioners in buildings where the civil service worked. This was key to public efficiency."

14 The majority of the new constructions in Singapore's Central Business District rely on transparent glass curtain walls as the primary surface envelope for the building, separating interior and exterior into discrete zones.

15 Riley, Terence. *Light Construction*, The Museum of Modern Art, New York, 1994.

16 See Colin Rowe and Robert Slutzky's influential text "Transparency: Literal and Phenomenal" from *Perspecta Journal* of 1963 for a reading of transparency as a spatial construct. Though Rowe and Slutzky develop and idea of layered space through time via painting, the possibility of a veiled space allowing for optical, spatial and atmospheric interpenetration simultaneously is not thoroughly discussed.

17 Fry, Maxwell, and Jane Drew. *Tropical Architecture in the Dry and Humid Zones*: Reinhold Pub. Corp., 1964. and Koenigsberger, Otto H, O. H. Ingersoll, and T. G. Mayhew. *Manual of Tropical Housing & Building*: Orient Longman Private Limited, 1975.

18 Herzog, Jacques. "Graduate School of Design Lecture." 5 May 2011.

19 Semper, Gottfried. "The Principle of Dressing Has Greatly Influenced Style in Architecture and in the Other Arts at All Times and among All Peoples." In *Style in the Technical and Tectonic Arts; or, Practical Aesthetics*, 242, 1860.

** For the avoidance of doubt, references to the term "Architect", throughout this text refer to the professional designation of the author as a State of New York, USA and State of Rhode Island, USA registered Architect and in no way does it imply that the author is registered as an "Architect" as defined by the Board of Architects in the Republic of Singapore. His role is as a design consultant for those projects located in the Republic of Singapore working in consultation with local Architects of Record.

Photo Credits

Unless otherwise indicated, all images and drawings are by the author.

Fig. 1   Picasso, *Les Demoiselles d'Avignon.* © The Museum of Modern Art/ Scala, Florence 2013, © Succession Picasso 2013

Fig. 2   Gertrud Arndt, *Mask Portrait No.16.* © Bauhaus-Archiv Berlin, © S.A.C.K

Fig. 3   Gertrud Arndt, *Mask Portrait No. 13.* © Bauhaus Archiv Berlin, © S.A.C.K

Fig. 4   Julio Le Parc, *Lunettes pour une autre vision.* © Adagp

Fig. 5   Julio Le Parc, *Instabilite.* © Adagp

Fig. 6   Bridget Riley, *Current.* © The Museum of Modern Art/ Scala, Florence 2013, © Bridget Riley 2013

Fig. 7   Bridget Riley, *Fall.* © Tate, London 2013, © Bridget Riley 2013

Fig. 11   Edward Durell Stone, *US Embassy Chancery and Staff Housing.* © Huffington Post

Fig. 12   Erwin Hauer, *Design 5.* © Erwin Hauer Studio

Fig. 13   Vladimir Ossipoff, *IBM Building,* Honolulu. © Adam Smith http://www.flickr.com/photos/army_arch/4437097918/

Fig. 14   Curtis & Davis, *United Steelworker.* © Tom Bastin

Fig. 15   James Ferrie and Partners, *AXA Life Building.* © Erik L'Heureux

Fig. 16   Le Corbusier, *Capitol Complex, The Secretariat.* © Peter Sheppard

Fig. 17   Oscar Niemeyer, *Edificio Copan.* © Tuca Vieira

Fig. 18   Geoffrey Bawa, *Kandalama Hotel.* © Scarlett Tu

Fig. 19   Le Corbusier, *Villa Shodan.* © Pavel Suprun

Fig. 20   Le Corbusier, *Ahmedabad Textile Mill Owners' Association House.* © Achyut Kantawala

Fig. 21   Louis I. Kahn, *Shaheed Suhrawardy Medical College Hospital.* © Naquib Hossain

Fig. 22   Charles Correa, *Kanchanjunga Apartments.* © Achyut Kantawala

Fig. 23   No.6 Goodwood Hill. © Epiphanie Lie

Fig. 25   Luigi Moretti, *Palazzina Il Girasole.* © Gabriele Basilico, © Fondazione MAXXI 2013

A Conversation

The following is a conversation
between Grit Vltavsky and Erik
L'Heureux during February and
March 2013. Grit Vltavsky is an
architect practicing in New York
City. To navigate space and time
difference, this conversation on veils,
architecture, and design research
was conducted via digital means.

—

*Grit   We have known each other
for over fifteen years, and you continue
to impress me with the rigor of your
research and design. The last five years
have been especially productive.
You are compiling an edited version
of your work under the title*
Deep Veils. *How do you evaluate
your work through writing about and
illustrating it? How does your work
contribute to academia and practice
alike? And how does the notion of
design research apply?*

Erik   People often find it difficult
to speak of their own work, myself
included—mostly because it not
only is rational but also depends on
intuitions, coincidences, and many
challenges. And then there is, of
course, the speed of the projects,
a long list of requirements,
and many demands from clients.
But regardless of these
circumstances, I have learned to
trust my intuitions to help me
synthesize my work. Foremost, it
preserves the serious intellectual
endeavor above the plethora of
project distractions or the default of
simply solving problems.

Paying attention to my intuition
does not mean a lack of seriousness
about research or focus on my larger
ambitions related to architecture.
On the contrary, each project has
become a part of a series of
explorations to serve a purposeful
thesis. *Deep Veils* is such an
undertaking, as it is comprised of
a series of investigations. Editing
these investigations is helping me to
slow down, curate, and calibrate the
design research I have been engaged
with over the past five years, though

I find traces of the research going back fifteen years—as long as I have known you. I am taking stock now, focusing the research, and making manifest the various modes in which this is tested in practice.

While I am articulating my projects in words, I am describing how I make architecture. Writing about it forms the intellectual foundations of my work. This synthesis will focus the next five years of my work even more precisely.

But you not only wanted to know about my intuitions and the process of writing; you asked about my design research. *Deep Veils* not only serves as a metaphor for architecture in the tropics, obviously for the building performance necessitated by the atmosphere, but also for a suggestion of another relationship between people, inhabited space, and views. A veiled architecture does not dissolve but rather gets in the way; it interferes specifically and precisely to enrich our experience of space. The ten projects shown here are different manifestations of my research on veils, translated into spatial and

material terms.

I am most interested in veils that change and adjust—not only literally (in terms of being operable), but also through permutations across their entire surface. Digital visualization and digital fabrication make the fabrication of these screens possible. I have found that the most successful envelope is one that is dynamic and serves multiple purposes—from optical to experiential to passive sustainable strategies. In that regard, *Deep Veils* has been influenced by my work in both academia and practice. And in turn, this research has contributed to teaching and building, thus making it part of the ongoing architectural discourse.

—

G   How are you organizing your work for this publication? Are you editing your presentation to highlight your architectural research on veils? Is there a method of analysis, investigation, concept study, presentation, and/or photographic representation that is especially tailored to your thesis?

E Representing my work is as important as the work itself. The representation is a product of the thinking that goes into the work, and offers another experience of it beyond the physical. The work is presented through a variety of traditional architectural devices: drawings, models, and photographs. However, drawings are an especially important device for communicating architectural thinking and research about the veil. I am employing three important drawing techniques: unfolded elevations, axonometrics, and exploded obliques. Each describes the research into veils in a very particular manner.

The most direct and obvious is the unfolded elevation. This drawing technique flattens an element, in this case the veil, into a continuous unwrapped surface. I often think about Marcel Duchamp's *The Large Glass*, because the work is situated between the two and three dimensional, between painting and experience, between transparency and interference. The unfolded veil, like a veil that one might wear, operates along similar lines. I hope to design a veil that is encompassing throughout the spatial experience, subtly changing along with the architectural space. For example, a veil wraps *A Simple Factory Building* in section. During the design development, an unfolded elevation of the veil helped me to refine the gradations of the opening sizes and the progression of the pattern along the different elevations.

Sectional worm's eye axonometrics prioritize the underside of canopies, overhangs, and interior volumes rather than elevation and roof alone. Here in the tropics, where shades and covers are especially important, drawing in this manner has forced me to think carefully about the navigation of exterior space and the resulting interior volumetric configurations. Sectional worm's eye drawings of the *Stereoscopic House* and *A Simple Factory Building* reveal the importance of large internal courtyards and their relationship to the surrounding volumes. In this case, looking up is more important than looking down. There are similar ambitions in Louis Kahn's worm's eye drawings of the Phillips Exeter Academy Library and the unbuilt US Consulate in Luanda, Angola. I am inspired by the magnificent drawings of Auguste Choisy, especially in how the light is brought into the interior spaces. My design has only profited by developing it through these projections. Many skylights and roof protrusions are direct results of changing my view point.

Likewise, exploded obliques reinforce operational components of my design, where elemental rules have immediate impact on the volumetric formation of the architecture. These drawings are almost like diagrams, though they are less reductive than the simplistic versions used typically in architectural concept studies. I employ these drawing techniques to investigate spatial relationships. By extension they have become a tool for elemental design research at the National University of Singapore. Two books I recently published, *Additions & Subtractions* (2008) and *Singles & Multiples* (2013), describe elemental operations in and on architecture.

Today, there are many discussions about the death of drawing due to the over-reliance on three-dimensional modeling and digital representation. These types of drawings, regardless of the tools with which they are produced, significantly clarify my thinking in architectural terms. This extends to the selection of photographs, the modes of model fabrication, and even the construction drawings. Usually the test of a project's coherence is if I can reduce the project, merging both plan and elevation into a tailored unfolded drawing. If all the surfaces can be formed into one great textile-like drawing, then I am very excited and intuitively know I am closer to design excellence.

—

G   To celebrate the Lunar New Year (Figure 30), you generated an interesting graphic. It is a repeating pattern of curves with what appear to be strategically placed in-fills.

Lines are amplitudes and in-fills are amorphous shapes. In the context of the Lunar New Year, this might symbolize the skin of a snake. It is not architecture, but very similar to your concept diagrams of three-dimensional wall cladding and/or exterior screens. Please tell me more about how you develop these patterns. Are they derived from abstracting a symbolic reference point? How do you transform a pattern into a three-dimensional application?

E   I developed the Lunar New Year graphic out of a simple "S", rotated and multiplied to produce a long undulating line. Stacking the line produced a field, a tessellated pattern that fills the graphic. The negative space of the pattern is selectively obscured to merge the boundaries between pattern and elemental "S". I have explored patterns similar to these in some of my projects over the past years, both as formal investigations into surfaces and for three-dimensional applications, such as interior and exterior screens. At times, I create patterns from a symbolic reference

point (in this case the year of the snake), which then stays embedded in the design as one level of interpretation. More often, these patterns are transformed from another origin into an architectural element, transcending their original meaning. In the realm of architecture, they may function as a shading or optical device.

In the *Stereoscopic House*, for example, the upper storey and attic-level volume are clad with two veils. One is timber in a herringbone pattern which is raised off the building. Operating as a rain and thermal screen, the timber at once unifies the differences between roof, wall, and ceiling, and minimizes the direct solar load onto the house. This is an important consideration when building one degree north of the equator. A second veil of perforated aluminum panel screens directs views during daylight hours and minimizes the intense western afternoon sun. The panels are operable and changeable to the sun path when more transparency is desired. The perforation pattern itself is adjusted over the west facade; areas of more perforation correspond to public areas of the house, while areas with less perforation indicate areas with privacy concerns. Laser cutting of the panels allowed each panel to be different.

A second project in which a patterned "deep envelope" is evident is *A Simple Factory Building*. Here, a deep trellis pattern sits proud of the window wall. The pattern is purposefully anamorphic, changing proportion and scale as it ascends the front facade. As seen most apparently in the section, the trellis wraps around the roof, the rear facade, and the car porch ceiling to perform a variety of roles. At times, it obstructs and interferes with views of the street, and at other times, especially at the upper levels, it opens to panoramic views of the surrounding landscape. Overall, the trellis assembly in Dryvit-coated polystyrene mitigates solar radiation on the building, allowing the expansive use of glass for natural lighting without the negative consequences this could have in the tropics. Without digital fabrication, this would not have been possible. Computer-controlled hot wire cutting allowed the ease of fabrication of the complex geometries of the pattern, as the edge profile is both substantially tapered and angled in section and plan.

Typically, in using patterns, I attempt to simplify the exterior surfaces to one or two that could be wrapped. Initially, I devise a variety of patterns, undertake modeling, and test deployments to ascertain impacts and effects while researching on a suitable material to fabricate these complex three-dimensional screens. I find optical artists such as Bridget Riley, Julio Le Parc, and Victor Vasarely inspiring. The works of these artists have a fascinating dynamic because they are deeply rooted in a methodical and reductive design process. Their works do not rely on composition, but on experience and optical effects. In that regard, the space is quite differently organized than the works of Piet Mondrian, for example. But in general, optical art, in the form of paintings and sculptures, is very different from my architectural work. I strive to develop patterns into three-dimensional devices and calibrate not only experiential, but also the functional and spatial requirements.

—

G   Most of your projects incorporate myriad veils, but the two projects you mentioned have especially intricate ones. You said that screens guide views from the interior and are important in the transmission of light. There is an extraordinary photo study of light streaming through a pattern of organic shapes into the Stereoscopic House, bouncing off curved and vertical planes, and creating an ephemeral choreography of bright spots filtered by a patterned veil. Could you explain further how you orchestrate these experiential effects?

E   All natural light has distinct characteristics. In the tropics, the light quality is very different from the Mediterranean or North American regions, such as New England where I grew up. Being in the equator, the sun's path is entirely consistent throughout the year.

The sun rises and sets at the same time each day and arcs directly overhead. The intensity of the tropical sun tends to wash things out; it has a bleaching effect on the atmosphere. It rains almost every day and shifting humidity levels alter the refraction of light rays. Here, capturing and creating dynamics of natural light through architecture is especially intriguing.

The veil produces a dynamic atmospheric quality as it offers thermal comfort and optical privilege. And it creates moving light patterns tracing the sun's path. I have worked with various techniques to achieve phenomenological effects. For the *Stereoscopic House* and *Pile Houses*, aluminum panels were cut into custom screen perforations with water-jets. These screens consist of a series of layers, each activated by ever-changing sunlight. When light projects onto oblique surfaces, flecks of light and shadow bring about distorted patterns. This ephemeral spectacle is delightful to observe. More than a casual side effect, it is an essential attribute of a purposeful veil.

Digital software is useful for investigating parameters of patterns and for fabricating complex geometries. Adobe Illustrator turns out to be a powerful design tool I currently employ to create pattern variations. These patterns are then projected in Rhinoceros and AutoCAD 3D to study three-dimensional effects. However, my emphasis is not on parametrics or finding perfect algorithms to craft patterns. I rather concentrate on the specific site conditions and functional program of the project. It is relatively simple to generate multiple veil options, but much more difficult to test these for performance, fabrication techniques, and budget limitations. Most often full-scale mock-ups are absolutely required to verify optical and experiential effects previously anticipated only in computer simulation.

If there is an underlying "formal approach", it is one of moving away from "composition" as an architectural strategy and toward tessellation, aggregation, and the creation of an architectural field that has performative and experiential effects. The use of gradients, stretching, and deformation are the underlying design operations. These design techniques are applied in the architectural trope of the veil and the aggregated volumes of the *Neighborhood Towers*. When all twenty-six *Pile Houses* are constructed, various roof forms should collectively produce a field of skylight and roof protrusions that unifies the entire neighborhood.

—

G   The way you speak about your work indicates a high level of research, both on an academic and professional level. How do you juggle design and research with practice and teaching at the university? Surely it requires great energy to marry project proposals with your design explorations. Do you think the challenges of building for clients has affected and improved your design? And how does teaching influence your work?

E   Naturally, practice informs my teaching and academic research, and being a teacher also enables me to view my design work as a form of research. There is a unique feedback loop here that improves the outcomes of both. The challenge lies in not making one role serve the other. Indeed, there is the old sterotype of giving students the same projects as those currently undertaken by an office. Rather, I try to develop parallel research strands that can inform one another in a complementary manner. For example, research in my second-year studios on geometry relate to the approaches I have in practice as well as my interests in aggregate forms, deep envelopes, and elemental geometries. In practice, the drawings of the *Pile Houses* and *Neighborhood Towers* have an analogous relationship with many of the works featured in my two books on geometry (prodigiously illustrated with student research): *Additions & Subtractions* (2008) and *Singles & Multiples* (2013). Extensive research on formal strategies of aggregation are done in teaching as well as in design practice, and traces of it can be found in both.

The Singapore National Pavilion at the 12th Venice Biennale (curated and designed with Khoo Peng Beng, Belinda Huang, and Florian Schaetz), merges the academy and practice most evidently. The research on deep envelopes led to the design of the gallery-like tube, while the research in my thesis-level studio on Singapore, density, and hydrology provided the content of much of the exhibition. Extended research of EIFS and Dryvit, being then deployed on *A Simple Factory Building*, supported the very production of the exhibition's material manifestation. It is a synthesis of the research produced in both practice and teaching. There are currently plans for the reconfiguration of the exhibition, titled *1,000 Singapores: A Model of the Compact City*, to be displayed in Paris in 2015. I look forward to extending both the academic and the practice-based research into these new contexts.

However, while the research may run in tandem and design concepts may overlap, the reality is that the work in the office always goes beyond my academic teaching. Practice requires the need to build and construct; questions on fabrication and detailing, site conditions, and client-driven programmatic requirements have to be resolved. Practice and academia have very different approaches to design research, hence only together may they offer the opportunity for comprehensive exploration.

—

G   When you speak about the Pile Houses, you describe them as a modular and methodical design project. They are also clearly extensions of your design research. At the same time, your work is deeply responsive to a specific site condition; hence you create unique designs with generic elements. How do you unite the modular and the singular? Is this a challenge that is particularly pertinent in your location?

E   Since I arrived in Singapore, I have been deeply intrigued by the country's embrace of the future, its amazing ability to change, and its singular determination to lead technical and scientific progress. It is a space of perpetual architectural development unlike anything I recall from my time in the USA. In my academic research here, I have taken this fascination to heart. Much of my work centers on Singapore itself, as a means of uncovering and making sense of this place I call home. This has resulted in a series of comparisons between Singapore and Dubai, Cambodia, Hong Kong, and Shanghai. There have been three research projects—"Singapore Transcripts", "Singapore Probes", and "Singapore Metropolitan Region"—all examining and making the multitude of forces that drive contemporary Asian urbanism.

This research has informed my urban-scale design work. Both *Neighborhood Towers* and the *Pile Houses* incorporate urban strategies that come out of my experience in Asia. For example, the pedestrian-scaled alleyway, the partially covered street, the walled perimeter, and the courtyard are all utilized to create urban environments that celebrate a different form of urbanism than the one I knew from my time in New York.

Neighborhood Towers breaks down the mass of a single podium into a multitude of small buildings linked by overhead passageways. This aggregation recalls the small neighborhoods found in Chengdu as well as my experiences in the alleys of Hong Kong, Shanghai, and Singapore. These become entirely productive and intensely used urban spaces—an important alternative to the "tower in the park" mode of urban design that has by now become little more than a tired formula.

Likewise, in the *Pile Houses,* the courtyard and perimeter wall interiorize private space, but at the same time create a unified urban neighborhood—a commonality and a form of social agreement as a foundation for neighborhood interaction. The variety of the second-storey volumes and roof profiles produces diversity in the field of consistency. There is no difference to the shophouse typology in Southeast Asia.

Practicing in Singapore is deeply rooted in the realities of building on the equator. The atmosphere is extremely hot, humidity is consistently high, and the sun shines and rain pours almost every day. Many clients demand air conditioning and the "temperatization" of tropical architecture. This cannot be avoided. The challenge is to design between these two states—one an entirely open, ventilated spatial experience and the other an entirely sealed mechanically modified atmosphere produced through the conditioning of air. I respond by employing passive design strategies to minimize solar loading on the building; introducing courtyards and spaces that ensure cross ventilation; and creating volumetric overhangs and double-layered facades to keep the sun away from the interior. The result is an architectural approach located between the open and closed, the symbolic and the performative, the mechanical and the sustainable.

In general, Singapore has been very generous—both as a site of investigation and a space in which to practice. The work is always evolving, though I am adapting and transforming my architectural vocabulary to be more adjusted to architecture on the equator. This primarily requires a fine-tuned approach to site, microclimate, atmosphere, sun, and shade. Architecturally, many of the devices or tropes that constitute temperate architecture don't work or have little relevance on the equator. It has been a learning process.

For example, the short-duration and very small project *Instant Pop-Up* appeared to be fairly solid, but it was actually punctuated by a variety of small openings that facilitated cross ventilation. The tops of the tapered trapezoidal roof forms were open, facilitating the evacuation of hot air. I would have preferred the skin to be even more porous; however, time, security, and budget demands required an expedient solution found in polycarbonate. This material was especially suitable for a project that was to last only a few months. *A Simple Factory Building* more

effectively solved the disjunction of a porous envelope with the functional demands of a sealed one. It facilitated the demand for an open exterior surface to mitigate solar loading, combined with the necessities of a sealed enclosure in a double-layered facade. Interestingly, in both projects the environmental impact of the buildings when torn down is minimal. Construction material is used sparingly and the structure is fully recyclable. In Singapore, the demand for high density creates an environment where there is a tendency for buildings to last only very short time periods. Durability and recyclability of my architectural work are new facets that I like to infuse into every detail.

—

G I have noticed that you often mention the notion of "calibration", with your architecture being adjusted to the tropical climate. It is abundantly clear that you carefully attune your work methods over time in response to context and program.

In what other ways does your location influence your projects?

E   The environmental demands for cross ventilation, porosity, and shade prescribe an urban language very different from that of closed urban blocks, sealed envelopes, and urban tightness as found in the temperate region. Here, an emphasis on objects separated from one another, perforations in plan through courtyards, alleyways, and setbacks create an entirely different urban environment. Yet this more open typology is being challenged by the demands for higher increasing populations, and the need for air conditioning. For example, in *A Simple Factory Building*, the terrace party wall configuration is reminiscent of the many row house configurations found all around the world. However, I tried to amplify porosity through a fully open ground floor. The building is raised off the ground to encourage cross ventilation. A four-storey courtyard and an open roof terrace assist in breaking down the mass into smaller volumes that

are easier to cross ventilate, shade, and naturally illuminate.

Having a practice based in Singapore also comes with the challenges of different cultures of business, especially in terms of clients and contractors. In many ways, I find practicing here more challenging when cultural sensitivities directly impact the design work. What I might consider small issues often become large drivers in the design due to client requests. Feng shui and specific cultural implications are always in the background, impacting the work. These ideas often clash directly with the conceptual approach to architecture that I try to bring. The challenge then is to incorporate both concept and cultural affinities into a cohesive whole.

The culture of building in Southeast Asia is entirely different from my American background. Builders typically utilize large quantities of unskilled workers hailing from Bangladesh, Thailand, and China. Given the labor practices, I have found it difficult to find and cultivate a high level of craftsmanship. I would argue that craftsmanship, as a valuable trade and livelihood, is hard to find here. Hence a tremendous amount of effort is put into quality control and ensuring that what is designed is in fact implemented with quality and care. The speed of design and construction is by factors of magnitude far greater than it is in the US. This creates an especially challenging environment to operate in. I have slowly reduced the size of and scope of my efforts, and there are two reasons why: firstly, to have more control over the design process, and secondly, to ensure that the quality I seek is indeed implemented. I see that a smaller, more nimble operation is able to take on those special projects that have greater impact. I must also thank the many Architects of Record, credited at the end of the book, who have greatly facilitated and navigated the design directions.

The general culture in Southeast Asia is forward looking. This creates an exciting environment in which to design, where more ambitious ideas

are seen in a positive light. I have had the good fortune to work on a number of challenging and enriching projects.

—

G   It is easy to see why you won several prizes for A Simple Factory Building. Drawings and photographs are testimony to a stunning facade. However, there is more to the building than the facade. Please discuss how you re-interpreted an architectural type: the courtyard building. How does the massing work in regard to the urban context and site specifics?

E   *A Simple Factory Building* is located between two conflicting realities. The demands of the environment for cross ventilation, porosity, and shade prescribe a very different urban language from that of closed urban blocks, sealed envelopes, and urban tightness, which are being encouraged by the Singapore Master Plan. Increasing urban densities, intensified land use regulations, and increases in allowable gross floor areas have all encouraged bigger, more compactly positioned buildings. This is the struggle that is going on now— between a dense urban environment, and one more reminiscent of a dispersed tropical landscape.

A Simple Factory Building is located in a terraced industrial area. With recent increases to the allowable GFA in Singapore, buildings can be much larger. In this context, we tried to reconcile a bigger building volume with porosity. This was done through a fully open ground floor and the breaking down of the overall mass into smaller volumes that are easier to cross ventilate, shade, and naturally illuminate. The section utilizes ideas found in much of the indigenous architecture of Southeast Asia; the raising of housing on short pilotis is common throughout the region to ventilate the underside of the building. Typically, the courtyard in plan is found in many traditional shophouses for ventilation and illumination of the interiors. *A Simple Factory Building* incorporates a courtyard in section. The vertical courtyard allows for atmospheric control and breaks the plan into two separate areas, encouraging different uses and the option of leasing to different tenants. Coupled with the trellis screen, the building incorporates lessons from its local context yet projects them into a new larger urban scale.

The trellis, of course, is found throughout Southeast Asia. Le Corbusier praised the "brise soleil" as one of his five modern building canons and incorporated the trellis into most of his design in India. While Southeast Asian trellises are traditionally timber, Le Corbusier utilized concrete. For *A Simple Factory Building*, I sought a material that had the performance of both timber and concrete. It should be lightweight and easy to fabricate (timber), yet resistant to the negative effects of the tropical climate and robust enough to mitigate the solar radiation (concrete). Fabricated in EIFS and coated with Dryvit, the veil is lightweight. Due to its materiality, it was possible to create a dynamic geometric pattern that fulfills a multitude of requirements from thermal performance, to optical control, to structural and technical demands.

—

G   Without a doubt, building in Southeast Asia has altered your architectural thinking. Your work has profited from designing for a challenging climate. How did you further develop your regional design strategies for your project Neighborhood Towers in Chengdu, China?

E   Chengdu has a unique climate of high relative humidity and mid-range temperatures, and often has grey skies. The city is going through a period of tremendous development with whole neighborhoods being demolished and replaced by large corporate projects and mass housing blocks. The design takes on both climates, atmospheric and building, with a critical and yet nuanced design approach. From an urban viewpoint, I appreciate the existing neighborhoods of small-scaled pedestrian streets and tight adjacencies between buildings found throughout the older sections of Chengdu. I absolutely believe that the social cohesion and dynamic city life produced by the aggregation of smaller buildings is something to be supported and amplified. It is really a wonderful city, especially where traditional fabric is still intact.

As such, the design for *Neighborhood Towers* has ten smaller buildings distributed throughout the site. There are also smaller buildings interlinked by public exterior walkways and alleyways, providing street frontage for storefront programs, shops, restaurants, and so on. At the pedestrian scale a vibrant social experience comes to life. For a government institutional building, its openness and porosity to the neighborhood and public are key attributes. Third- and fourth-level bridgeways link all of the ten buildings to each other and to the two main towers, allowing for a continuous interior circulation.

The two large spec office blocks sit among the smaller buildings, and share a similar architectural vocabulary. Grey brick elliptical scoops are removed from the corners of the buildings as they meet the street level, each providing a larger courtyard-like space at the intersections of the ground-level alleyways. A continuous trellis wraps around all of the twelve buildings, reflecting light onto the floor slabs as a means of promoting natural illumination. The trellis pattern, a variant to that on *A Simple Factory Building*, is scaled in a gradient creating an optical effect on the volumes without the normative clues of building scale. The intent is not to produce disorientation, but rather to focus the orientation onto the pedestrian and public passageways at the street level. Of course, practicing in China requires a particular patience; but still I hope that the groundbreaking of the project will commence shortly.

—

G *You mentioned that buildings in Singapore are erected and torn down quickly. This may contradict your LEED (Leadership in Energy and Environmental Design) training, but it has urged you to develop ways to integrate reusable materials into your designs. How does LEED contribute to your work?*

E Singapore's rapid rate of change means buildings often go through a process of "en-bloc" redevelopment. Buildings, even those just a few years old, are torn down to facilitate increased building densities and redevelopment. Typically, a thirty-year life span is the norm for Singapore's buildings, and some are much shorter, ten years being not unheard of. To negotiate this dilemma, I have been looking at reusable and recyclable materials, as well as methods of design that encourage reuse. The first component of reuse is durability; not just material durability but spatial durability. Simple, adaptable floor plans allow a building to be reconfigured easily, helping to ensure its ability to adapt to future uses. The strategic location of the fixed structure, egress, and common facilities allow for maximization of adaptable spaces. Having plenty of experience in interior architecture, I attuned planning for future change. In *A Simple Factory*

Building, for example, the floor plates were kept open with a basic core running along the west facade. By allowing the core to meet an open ground floor, there is more flexibility to move up and down the core and from front to back. Landlords could easily fit sub-divisions into the open plan and a front and rear tenant could potentially occupy the building. Even though this was not an immediate request of the client, I felt it was important that the building be ready for future changes.

I have been working with aggregate volumes that are simplified structurally and programmatically. The smaller volumes, when aggregated, are actually more adaptable and more likely to be durable for future use. First introduced in *A Simple Factory Building*, I continued this approach of flexible interior design to the *Pile Houses*. In *Neighborhood Towers*, the aggregate expression is more pronounced, making it a fundamental element of the layout.

Over time, I have slowly simplified the material palette.

I find that working with fewer materials produces a more coherent and rigorous project. In Singapore specifically, the constant temperature and relative humidity actually allows simple wall assemblies. Fortunately I can avoid assemblies with the tremendously complicated petroleum membranes or adhesive products often required with large temperature swings. Recycling a simple wall assembly is much easier, especially when containments are kept to as few locations as possible. Even concrete can be broken down for recycling as long as the petroleum is kept away. Likewise, aluminum, glass, and the polystyrene facade may be neatly separated for reuse. I estimate that about 98% of *A Simple Factory Building* could be recycled here in Singapore. For some new projects, I am eliminating plastic laminates altogether. It is a small but important design decision to keep the materials simple, natural, and recyclable; not to mention more cost effective.

As concrete and brick are the most common building materials in Singapore, I have explored the casting of concrete utilizing recycled timber pallets for formwork. The entire ground floor of *A Simple Factory Building* is built this way. Even the upper floors are simple 4 x 8-foot (1.2 x 2.4-meter) plywood off-form castings. The factory is an industrial building, hence the casting can be purposefully rough with formwork texture shown as an explicit design element. In *Neighborhood Towers*, I used the local grey brick found throughout Chengdu. For *A Simple Brick Interior*, solid bricks were a cost-effective way to achieve a screen. Being painted bone white, the homogeneity of the screen becomes legible. In the *Pile Houses*, I rendered the ground floor entirely in locally sourced homogeneous tiles. Thanks to a simple tonal difference between tile batches and the selection of two finish options, this approach could yield an effect much like granite, albeit without the material consumption, cost, and pollutants required to ship the material. Reflecting on all the work, my intent is clearly to take advantage of local building materials, and to deploy them most effectively and with the possibility of reuse if need to be.

LEED concepts are always present in the work, though as you noted, not necessarily applicable. The economic incentives and demands are very different in Singapore than the US. In light of the building differences, evaluation of success is not necessarily in following LEED concepts. I rather develop construction strategies that work in the current building culture and teach sustainable approaches which may lead to energy and water conservation, material reuse, and long-lasting structures adaptable for future needs.

—

G   Thank you for explaining your thesis about Deep Veils. *Your design research has brought about extraordinary work. At the same time there is much more to explore. In which direction will you pursue your research to deepen and extend your ideas?*

E   I am very much looking forward to seeing the *Pile Houses* project completed to test my hypothesis. Essentially, there are three types of veils that have constituted much of my research of late. These are variable perforations in two-dimensional surfaces; three-dimensional veils that read as a contiguous whole; and three-dimensional veils that are fabricated with many smaller pieces where there is ambiguity between the whole and its parts. Even though I just differentiated three types, all these are still under the umbrella of one research project. All the work in the office is dedicated to the overarching research, while simultaneously refining a subset of envelope characteristics. In that regard, I have focused my exploration, limited the number of variables (such as color and material), and generally honed my investigative process to control, guide, and focus the results.

There are two directions in which I wish to extend the research in the future. One is structural; the other is at the urban scale.

Of course, both extensions require larger projects and ones of more inherent complexity. I have already sketched a few ways in which the structural demands of architecture could be transformed into a self-supporting "deep veil". For example, the multitude of supports throughout a veil's design could transform into a structural system, transferring and carrying loads with efficiency and "economy of means". Of course, to launch this investigation a talented team and further simulations would be necessary. With each additional performance requirement upon the veil, the more sophisticated becomes the integration and systematic thinking to pull it off. But having talked about my intuition at the beginning of our interview, I cannot stress enough my confidence that my work with "deep veils" could be infused with structural concepts. Thereby, it would build upon my thesis and expand its impact on my academic underpinnings.

The second direction is testing the veil metaphor as part of the urban experience. At this scale, veils would have a greater spatial dimension, as spaces to inhabit and experience. I just scraped at the surface of this idea with *Neighborhood Towers*. Much more design research is needed to explore how many types of layers and spatial envelopes could be integrated into public and private realms. In my mind, "deep veils" could perform atmospherically and structurally, impacting the urban environment in sustainable and socio-economic ways.

Regarding my design research into "deep veils", I intend to measure against a comprehensive goal: to develop veils with a myriad of architectural functions that can be applied over a large surface and/or substantial volume, and be integrated into and completely alter perception and experience. It has been a fascinating undertaking, especially since the complexity of the research is ever increasing, but at the same time I already find that the most successful veil is one that is minimal in design, distilled to its inherent essence, simple and definitely reductive.

Thank you.

1 Singapore
2 Venice Biennale
3 Neighborhood Towers

Stereoscopic House

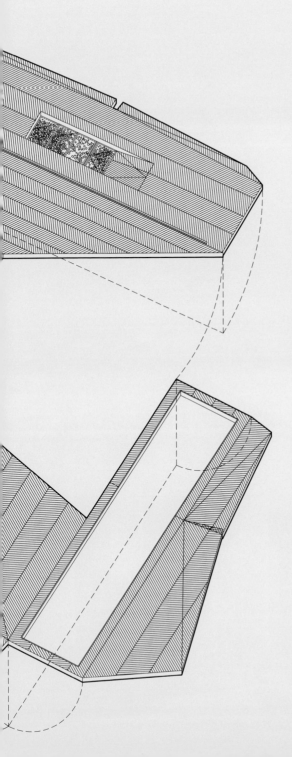

Location——Singapore
Area——708.8 m² / 7629.5 sf
2007–2011

Stereoscopic House

How can the veil be used to test the relationship between two and three dimensions? Can it perform thermally as well as optically? To what degree can the veil encourage a phenomenological experience?

Located on the flat reclaimed landscape of Sentosa Island in the Singapore Straits, the Stereoscopic House is sandwiched between the ocean (a "natural" view), a golf course (an "artificial" view), and two neighboring units that are just two meters away on the left and right. The architecture, designed and built between 2007 and 2011, manipulates the relationship between environment, waterscape and landscape, and view through four levels of optical and thermal calibration. The architecture addresses the issue of a tight site close to adjacent neighbors and demands for floor areas which led to a stacked approach.

The basement plinth, clad in travertine, contains various support functions for the house. A series of curvilinear skylights bring illumination into this lower level while permitting glimpses of the levels above. The central courtyard, which is open to the full four levels of the house, ventilates the basement and the upper floors and allows visual connection between the floors.

The main living level, situated on top of the basement plinth, is surrounded by translucent channel glass and transparent sliding windows. The sliding windows allow the level to be given various states of openness and closure. Cross ventilation and natural illumination can be maximized. When so desired, the entire wall can be opened, allowing the inside to transform into an exterior space. Alternately, it can be closed for the mechanical ventilation of the space. The living and dining areas front the sea, offering a panoramic view while being protected by the overhanging volume above.

The second and third storeys "float above" the living level and are encapsulated in a timber-surfaced tube. Within the tube are five bedrooms that are isolated from the adjacent neighbors, while precisely framing dramatic views of the ocean beyond in a stereoscopic manner. Two bedrooms on the second floor look to the sea, while also facing each other across a shared terrace that bifurcates the house. Two additional bedrooms share space within the house. One faces a golf course view through a screened verandah, and the other one is embedded into the center of the house. Angular roof-pitch codes shaped the dramatic framing of a view to neighboring islands from the third-storey guest bedroom. From there, looking out to the sea is a perfectly framed experience. The guest bedroom overlooks an elongated exterior terrace; the view forward is extended, while views left and right are completely obscured.

Setback regulations and roof codes demanded deformation of the tube in plan and section; a design approach of deep angular overhangs and large verandas resulted, which reduce solar radiation on the living spaces. In response to the tropical climate of Singapore, a layer of ironwood timber is wrapped over and merges the roof, side elevations, and ceiling of the upper levels while minimizing solar radiation transfer. In a herringbone configuration, the wrapper ventilates and breathes through its surface. Combined with perforated aluminum screens, the wrapper operates as both an optical and performative veil, calibrating view and temperature.

Diffused and reflected sunlight brightens interior spaces via angular skylights on the roof. Operable screens (cut with the water jet technique) allow the house to oscillate between opaque and transparent, closed and open, sealed and ventilated as an extension of the veil metaphor. Together, these additions and subtractions of volumes not only facilitate natural daylighting, but also create a phenomenological experience of light and shadow that is unique to the house.

Low-E glazing, solar water heating, extensive cross ventilation, rain harvesting systems, and evaporative cooling are combined with the typologies of the colonial verandah, Singapore shophouse courtyard, and Malay breezeway in a composition of form and environmental function—a reinterpretation of the Vanna Venturi House where the front, the back, and the sides all take on differing configurations in response to meaning and symbol as well as performance and experience.

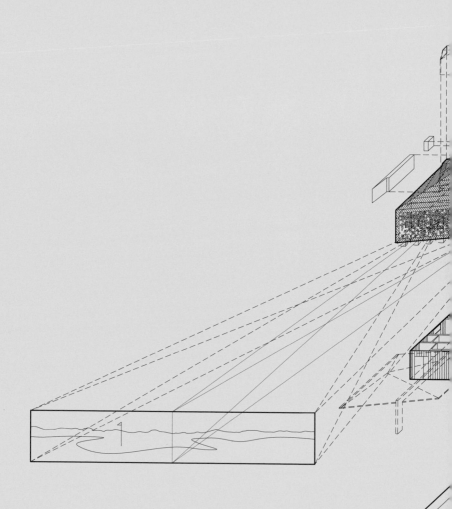

Eploded oblique

0   10

1

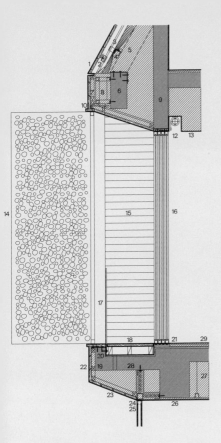

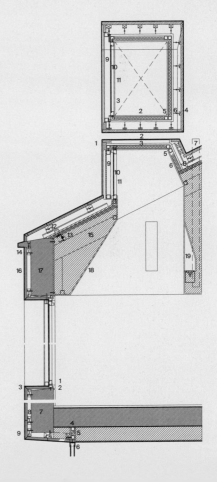

Detail Wall Section

1	25mm IPE Timber Roof Clad	15	Timber Wall Panel Cladding
2	Timber Clip Support	16	Sliding Door 17
3	Lysaght Roof Assembly		20mm Glass Balustrade
4	Metal C-Purlins Roof Support	18	25mm Timber Floor
5	Metal Roof Truss	19	50x50mm Battens
6	RC Beam	20	Glass Balustrade support
7	50x100mm Timber battens	21	18mm Timber Floor Internal
8	Metal Hollow Section Support	22	25mm IPE Timber Clad
9	RC Beam	23	25mm IPE Timber Ceiling Clad
10	25mm Timber Nosing End Piece	24	Metal Hollow Section Support
11	Metal Bracket for	25	Chanel Glass
	Perforated Panel Door	26	Gypsum Ceiling
12	Roller Blind	27	Ceiling Grid Support
13	Gypsum Ceilng	28	RC Slab
14	Aluminum Perforated Panel	29	Protective Screed

Skylight Roof Detail

1 100 mm Timber end Piece
2 Lysaght Roof Assembly
3 Spandek Metal Roof Clad
4 25mm IPE Timber Roof Clad
5 Metal Hollow Section Support
6 80kg Rockwool Insulation
7 25mm IPE Timber Roof Clad
8 Metal Flashing
9 Aluminum Perforated Panel
10 Aluminum Window
11 Aluminum Frame
12 Clip Support for fixing Timber
13 Metal C-chanel Roof Support
14 100mm Timber End Piece
15 Metal Roof Truss
16 Timber Cladding
17 RC Beam
18 Gypsum Ceiling
19 Light Housing

Wall Detail

1 50mm Aluminum Frame
2 Plastering End Cap
   with 10mm Grove line
3 Stainless Steel End Cap
   for Timber Alignment
4 Metal Hollow Section
   Support for Window
5 Aluminum Window Frame
6 9mm thk. Gypsum Ceiling
7 RC Beam
8 50x100mm Solid Timber
   backing Support
9 25mm IPE Timber Clad

0   1

0.2

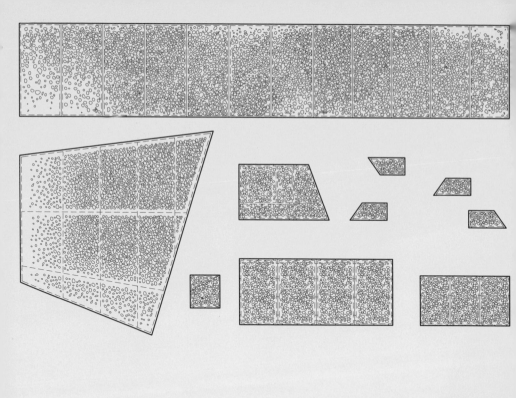

0   1
0.2

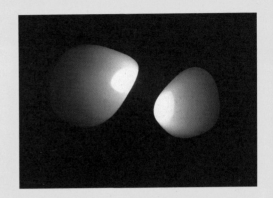

Detail Skyline Section

20mm thk. Tempered Glass
8mm Homogenous Tile
Plastered Wall
Chanel Glass
Travertine Stone Floor
RC Slab
Loose Stone Drain
Gypsum Ceiling
RC Perimeter Wall

10   Gypsum Curved Ceiling
11   Ceiling Grid Support
12   Build-up wall, CNC profile
13   External Drain
14   18mm thk. Timber Floor on
       Suspended Plywood Substrate
15   Waterproofing Membrane
16   Gravel Base
17   20mm Plastering

0   1

0.2

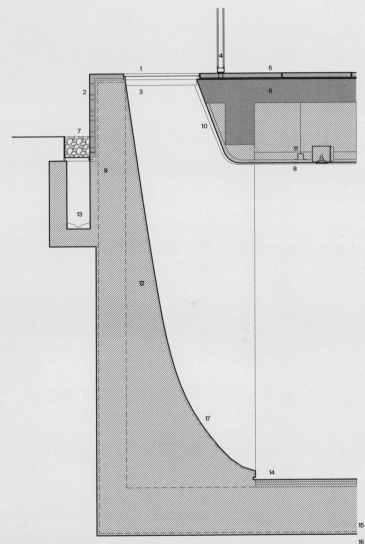

West elevation

Cross section

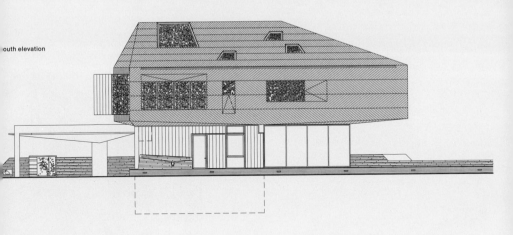

South elevation

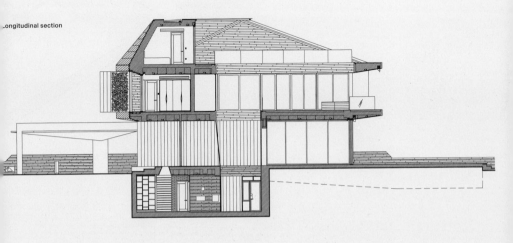

Longitudinal section

0   10

1

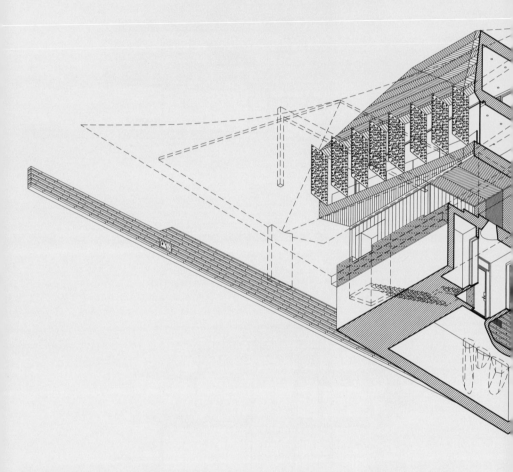

0   5

1

Worm's eye sectional axonometric

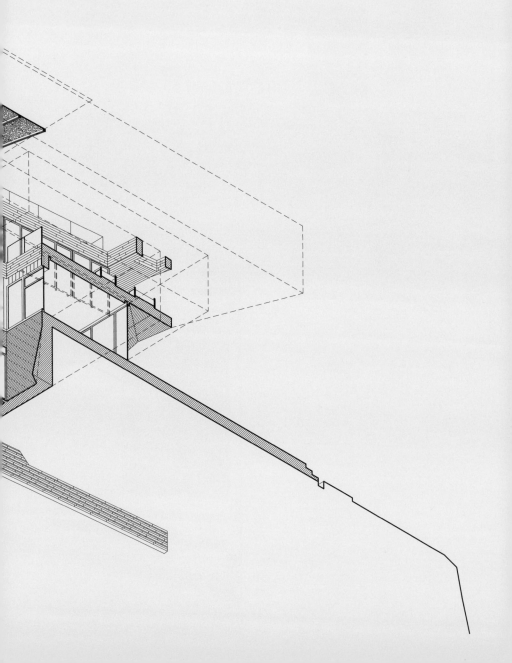

1st floor

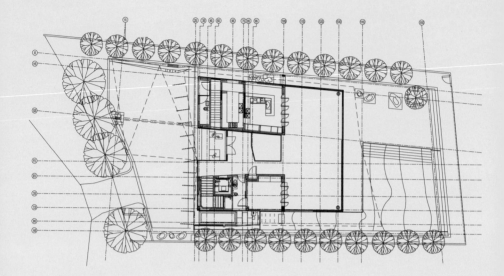

Basement

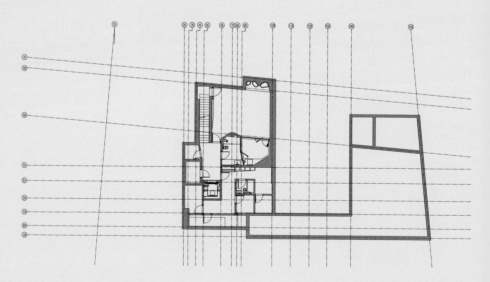

nd floor

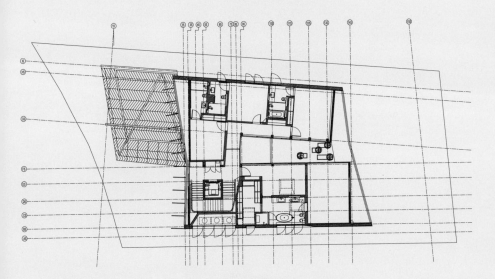

Attic

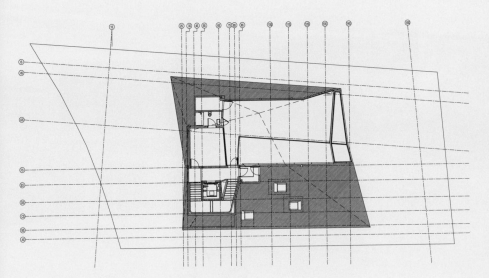

N

0   1   10

0

100

10

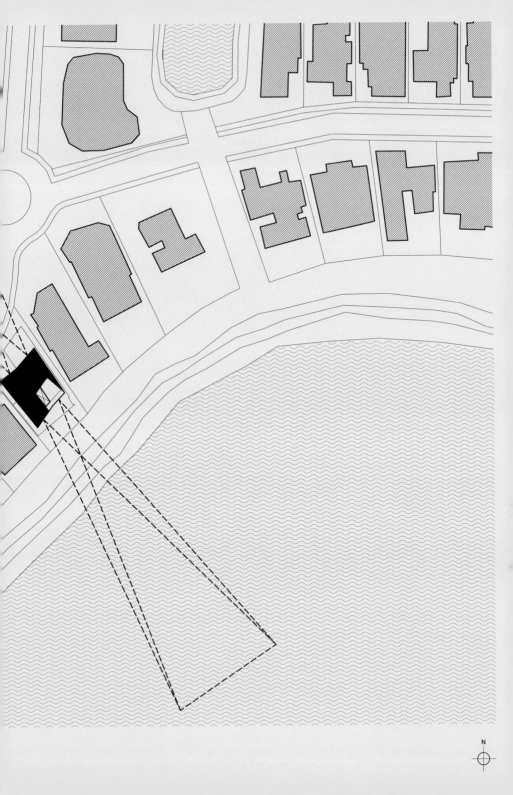

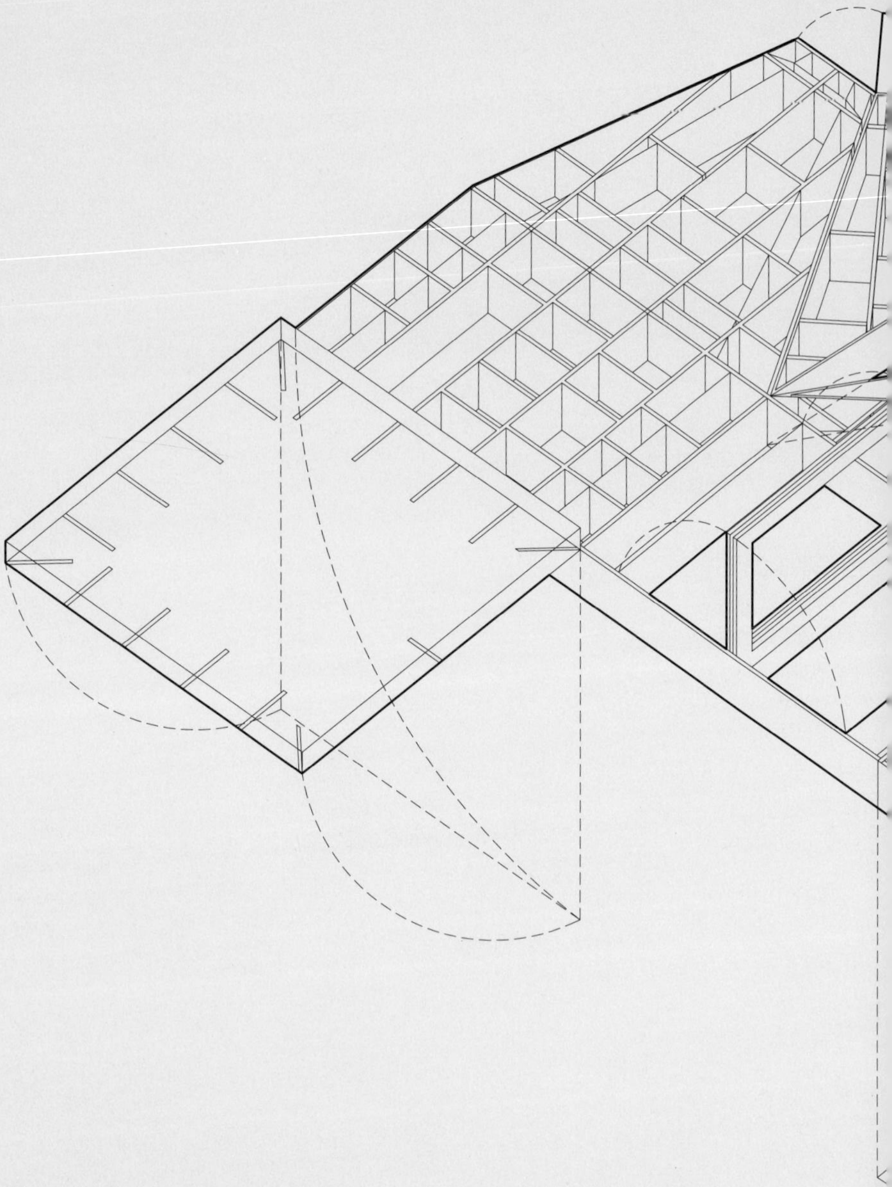

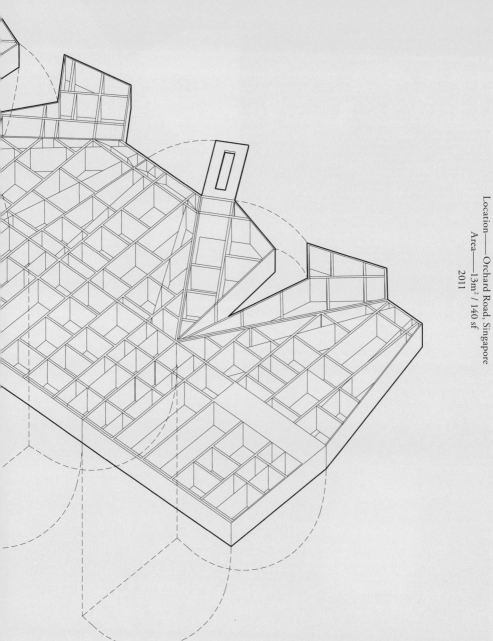

Location——Orchard Road, Singapore
Area——13m² / 140 sf
2011

Instant Pop-Up

Can the performance of the veil be enhanced when it is composed of two layers? How many functions can it deliver?

Instant Pop-Up (Popped Out by Inhabit) was a temporary 215-square-foot (20-square-meter) piece of architecture designed, built, and then removed between November 2010 and March 2011. It was located prominently on Singapore's main shopping street, Orchard Road. Two pyramidal volumes intersected about and shared the same plan configuration. The overall volume oscillated between elemental and complex, simple and dramatic.

Painted plywood shelving offered the necessary display spaces, holding clothes, shoes, accessories, and perfumes at the lower levels. Above, the plywood formed the trapezoidal structure of the dynamic roof forms. Openings were strategically located to facilitate cross ventilation, stack-effect cooling, security, and the evacuation of heat. Shelving was angled and open to the exterior for positive ventilation at the top of the roof forms, as well as at three corner locations at the lower levels. Two large doors were positioned centrally along the southern elevation, facing outwards to capture and direct prevailing microclimate breezes. The exterior, clad in inexpensive polycarbonate, provided rain protection and security, doubling as a light-diffusing and light-absorbing veil.

During the day, the architecture is read as a thickened white volume. In the evening, it transformed into an illuminating lantern. The veil was found here in two incarnations: one thick and one thin. The thick veil encompassed the vertical and horizontal shelving components that structured the space. This trellis-like scaffolding not only contained the program (the display and selling of merchandise), but was also calibrated to the climate. The thin veil of polycarbonate refracted and diffused the light, interfering with the view of the merchandise through translucency, while at the same time producing an attraction via its illuminating optical quality.

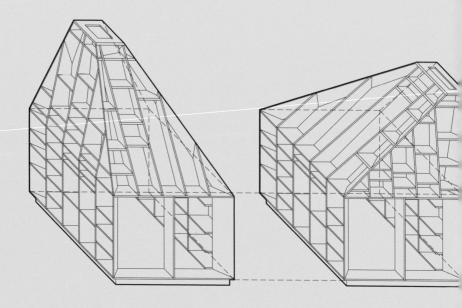

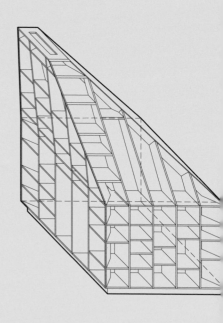

0   2.5

Exploded oblique   0.5

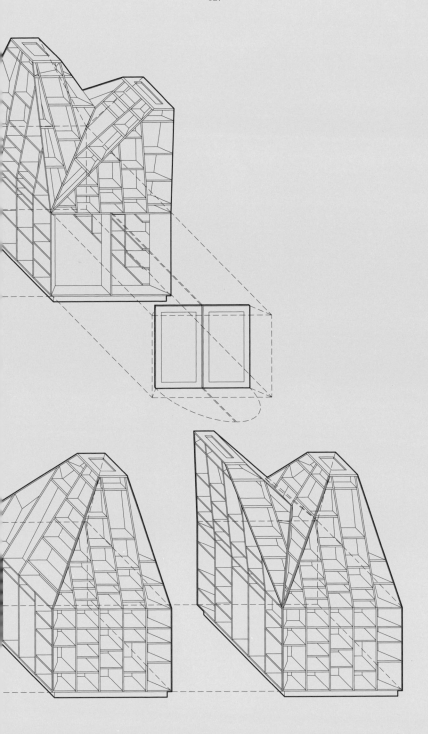

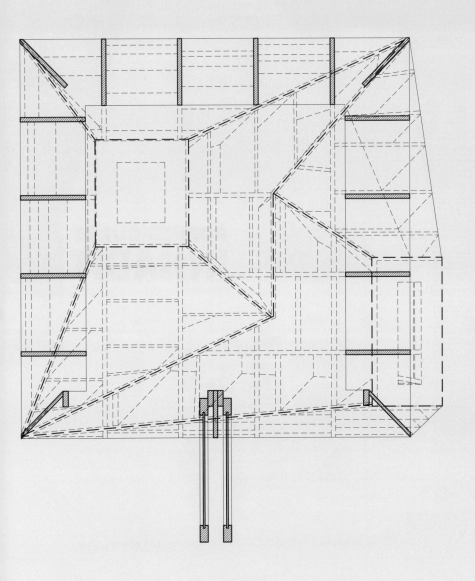

Ian

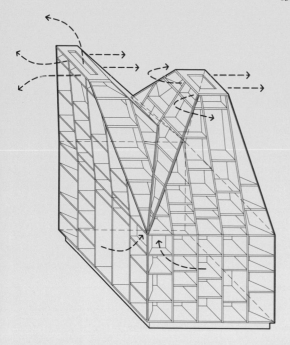

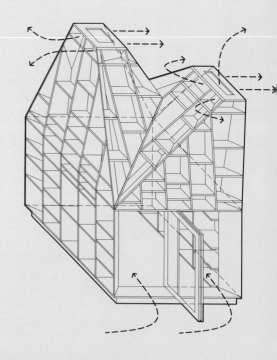

Environmental oblique

0   2.5

0.5

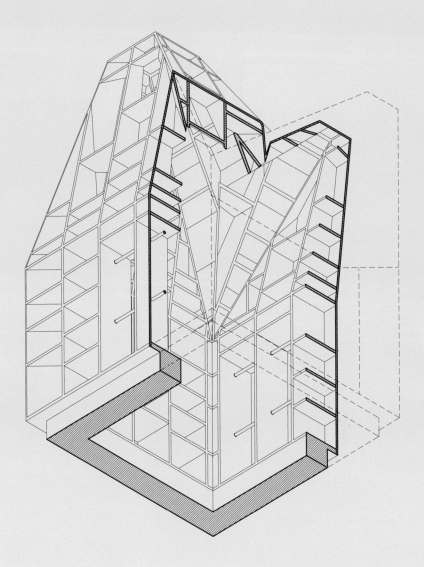

Worm's eye sectional axonometric

0   1

0.2

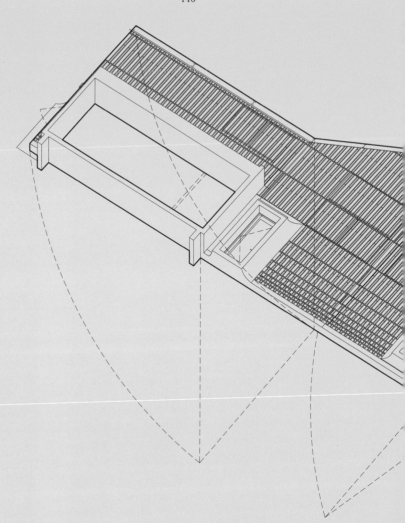

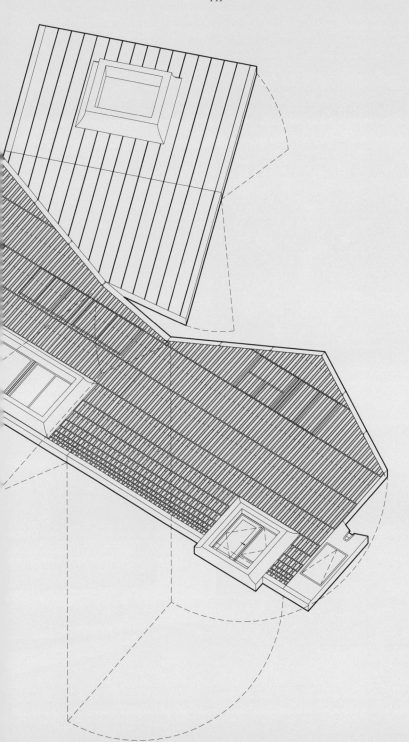

Location——Cornwall Gardens, Singapore
Area——275.8 m² / 2968.7 sf
2013–2014

Hut House

How can a veil be the entire elevational surface of an architecture? Can it be reductive to the point that there is only the veil as the architectural body itself?

A small hut-like addition of 1,560 square feet (145 square meters) to an existing landed residential property in the Holland Village neighborhood of Singapore is composed of a continuous EIFS thermal veil carved in relief. This 10-inch-thick (250-millimeter-thick) surface mitigates thermal heat gain while producing a delightful pattern of light and shadow. The pattern across the facade is stretched along the vertical axis, denying the normative conventions of scale to the two-storey object. Windows behind the veil are positioned to differing alignments and sizes, reinforcing a play of position and scale to undermine any registration of scale about the volume.

    The veil itself covers opaque and transparent surfaces alike, rendering the architecture as a discrete, almost toy-like object. Four specific protrusions—two for the entrance and the exit, one for the skylight, and one for an unobstructed view— extend beyond the veil in a form that appears to be stretched and pulled. These disruptions are fabricated in the same material as the veil; only the shape and use are changed. Various other windows needed for natural illumination are faced with operable screens in the same veil pattern allowing ventilation, light, and view without the normative disruptions to the architectural facade.

    Limited site area and setbacks transform the idealized hut form, carving it obliquely in plan, and thus creating a dramatic crystalline-like volume. Within, a bedroom and living room extension are found on the ground floor. A painting studio and gallery are found on the second storey, bathed in a veiled light quality as it is illuminated while protected from the heat and glare of intense tropical sun. A simple yet generously scaled interior stair wraps about the interior chamfered walls, merging the various levels. Sandwiched by an 8-inch (200-millimeter) floor line and roof line, the hut house works with reduction as an architectural concept—reduction of materials, tones, and volumetric complexity—to amplify the presence of the veil.

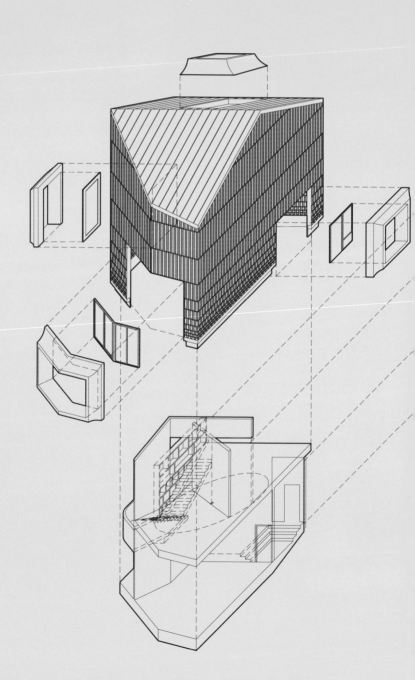

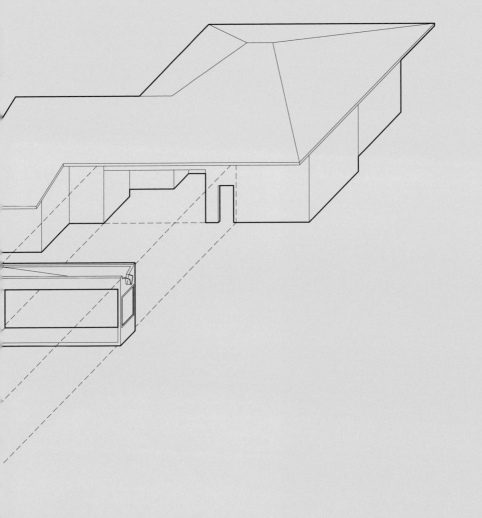

exploded oblique

0   1   5

2nd floor

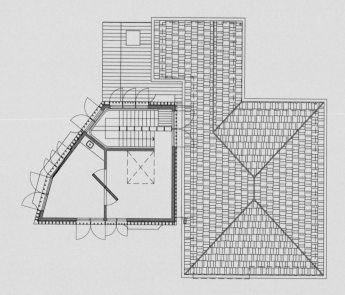

1st floor

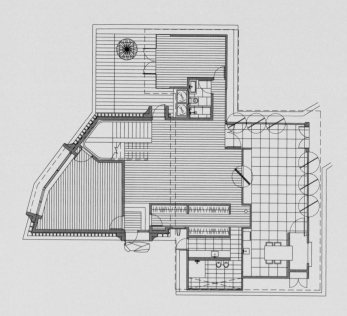

of

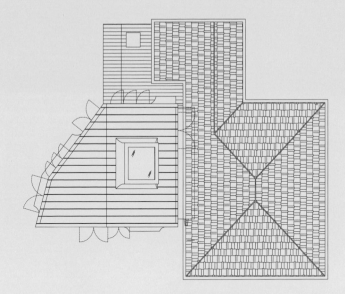

ngitudinal section

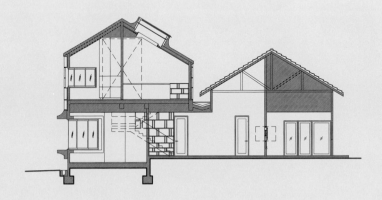

N

0   5
1

0   100

10

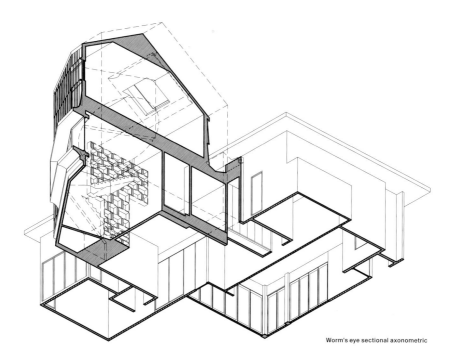

Worm's eye sectional axonometric

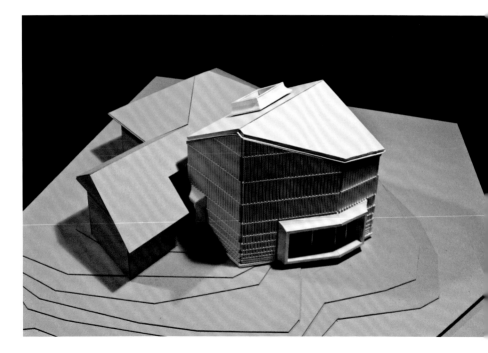

South elevation

West Elevation

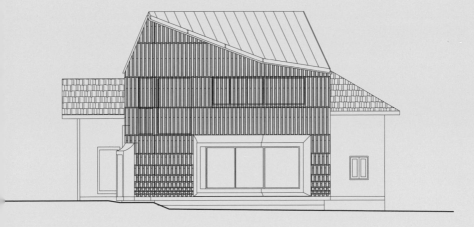

Detail Wall Section

1   50x50mm aluminum plate
      fastened to standing metal roof
2   Two layer masterclad with
      water proofing membrane
3   150x150mm H.S. section
      with flush purlins
4   3x100mm aluminum drip
5   Aluminum sub frame window
      header's sill
6   Aluminum low E glazing sliding
      windows
7   25x75mm aluminum operable
      screen
8   Pneumatic struts
9   250mm EIFS CNC cut to profile
10   Continuous waterproofing
      membrane
11   RC wall assembly
12   Perimeter drain
13   Plywood pelmut with
      concedled black out curtain

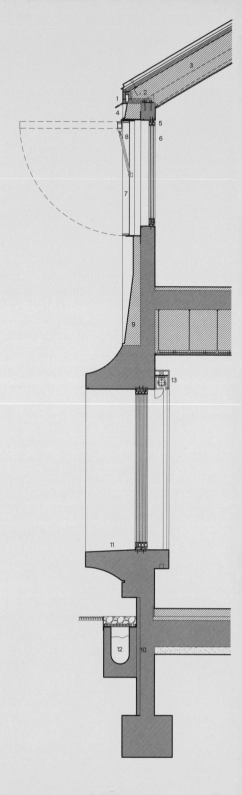

0   1

0.2

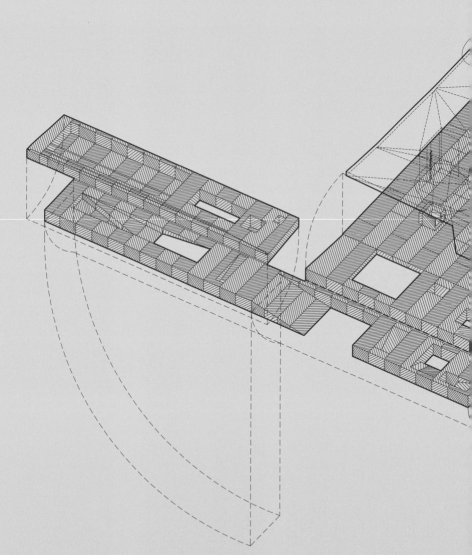

Canopy/Container

Location——Mandarin Gallery, Singapore
Area——177m² / 1905sf
2010

INHABIT
The Other Store

Canopy
Container

Can the veil be a site of tension? How can perforations in the veil affect experience, and perhaps behavior?

This 2,300-square-foot (213-square-meter) interior was designed and built in 2010 as a flagship store for a reputable independent fashion retailer (Inhabit) along Singapore's Orchard Road. The design resolves the problems of an extremely low ceiling height (2.6 meters) and limited storefront visibility due to the unit's corner location. As an introverted container wrapped in opaque herringbone-patterned oak, the design inverts normative expectations of large glass window displays. The oak appears consistently on both horizontal and vertical surfaces, extending the reach of, what is traditionally, a floor pattern.

A large white unadorned ceiling canopy, faceted in section, is set tight to the existing plenum level while forming three suspended dressing rooms below. Positioned around a central space, the dressing rooms create an interior living room, perfect for the performance of chatting, comparison, and gossip—the often neglected performances played out in the act of shopping. Floating off the floor, each dressing room is partially covered with large mirrors, providing and amplifying alternate views throughout the interior. A series of curvilinear subtractions in the white canopy violate the privacy of each dressing room, allowing a peep-like view from the public to the private realm. Likewise, 8-inch (200-millimeter) gaps above the floor reveal the shoes of the undressing inhabitants, further merging private and public zones while also functioning as air conditioning return ducts.

Recessed uplights in the herringbone container illuminate the ceiling and interfere with the retail experience at specific moments.

Small openings on the exterior of the container allow discrete views between the interior and exterior, yet they too are obstructed by angled, highly reflective glass. The design purposefully heightens the tension between the canopy and the container, the interior and the exterior, the clothed and unclothed. Though the metaphor of the veil is less apparent in its architectural manifestation as a screening device, indeed the design interrupts and interferes with the normative performance of shopping—an immensely optical act. In essence, the design purposefully addresses the shoppers and their retail experience to amplify and expose the codes of shopping, consumption, and retail architecture.

0

5

1

xploded oblique

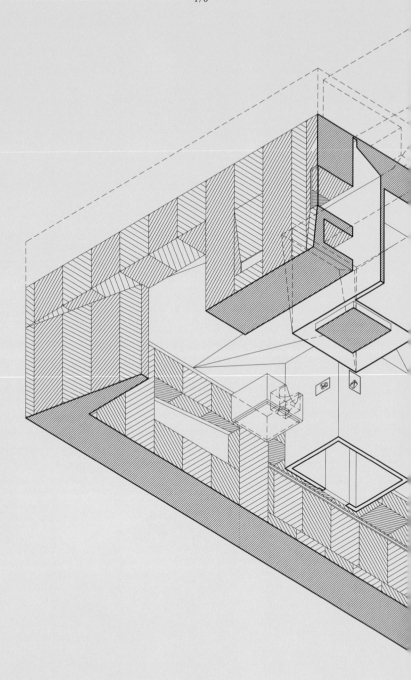

Worm's eye sectional axonometric

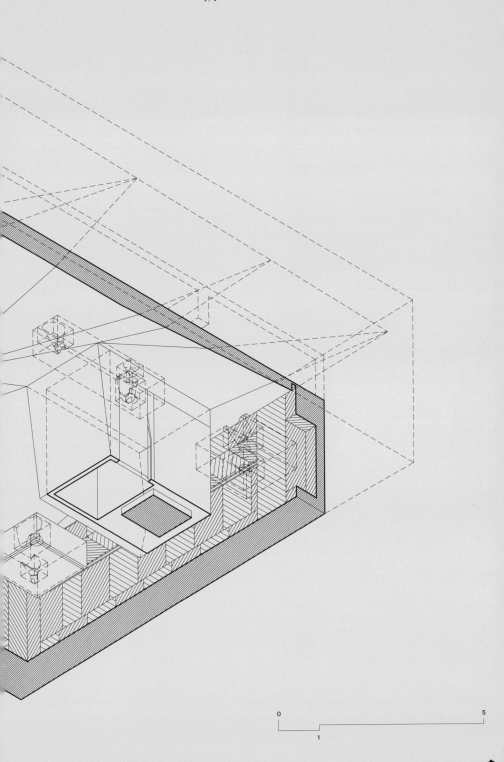

0   5

1

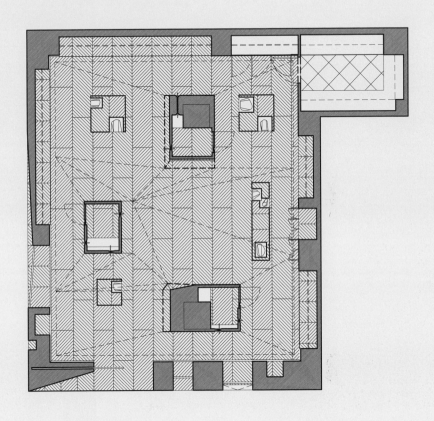

an

0
1

5

N

Suspended Wall Assembly

1   12mm gypsum board
    on metal studs
2   6x6 mm reveal with Z-bead
3   EIFS CNC cut to custom profile
4   40x350mm diameter brass tube
5   25mm T&G smoked oak
    planks on 18mm plywood with
    20mm screed

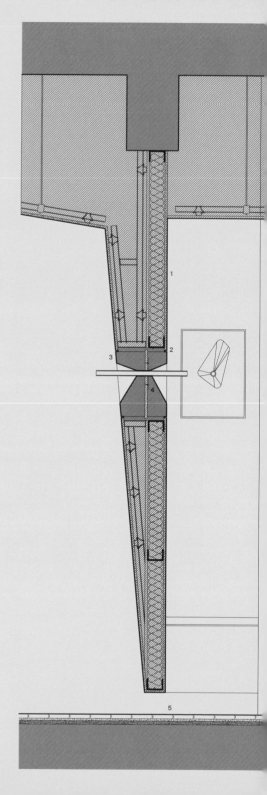

0   0.5

0.1

Location———Ion Orchard, Singapore
Area———113 m² / 1216 sf
2009

Location———Marina Bay Sands, Singapore
Area———288 m² / 3100 sf
2011

Deep Envelopes

Can the veil organize while it directs movement? Can it allow the retail experience to be controlled?

The term "Deep Envelope" describes two retail interiors for The Wright Gift in Singapore. One is situated on the uppermost level of the ION Orchard shopping center (2,000 square feet or 185 square meters), and the other one is located at The Shoppes at Marina Bay Sands (2,210 square feet or 205 square meters). The design language for both locations is predicated on the production of a flexible architectural screen and storage device that can organize a massive quantity of retail goods (gift items), while amplifying the codes of retail design. The intention was to minimize distraction and heighten the visual focus on each item held within the screen.

 The screen, calibrated to meet various demands, operates as a sectional wrapper that merges the walls and the ceiling into a continuous surface and pattern. At the wall, the screen creates deep pockets—window displays of sorts that highlight the items in the collection. At the ceiling, shallow pockets organize areas for lighting, air conditioning, speakers, and sprinklers. The depth of the wall surface is used as a device for obscuring and frustrating visual access to the collection. The idea is that by creating an experience where one must walk through the space to view each item, desire will be amplified. This interference is deliberate; it intensifies the presence of the architecture in a carefully controlled relationship between architecture display and object. The interiors were fabricated in anigre veneer, architectural-grade plywood, ivory lacquer panels, and stainless steel. The materials' subtle tones contrast purposefully with the retail items.

A custom herringbone American oak threshold clads the storefront and mediates the existing timber material and pattern of the public corridor, creating a surface of continuity while framing the anigre wrapper. LEDs, halogen downlights, and metal-halide fixtures impart a dramatic and ambient illumination, highlighting the quality and uniqueness of each gift while heightening the spatial experience.

The architectural system accommodates various site configurations. At The Shoppes at Marina Bay Sands, the long rectilinear deployment tapers in section, creating a long funnel. This exaggerates the perceived length of the space, amplifying one's impression of the collection's size. Likewise, at ION Orchard, the architectural system bends along a crooked plan. Compressed around the turning point, the close proximity of vertical elements creates a sweeping and twisting effect. The curved plan of the retail space is highlighted by two massive center-pivoted doors. Constructed with machined stainless steel and translucent Panelite, each door performs as a plane that directs views and circulation. Likewise, five highly crafted self-illuminated Panelite doors at the rear of the store camouflage storage while providing a dramatic interior façade within the store proper.

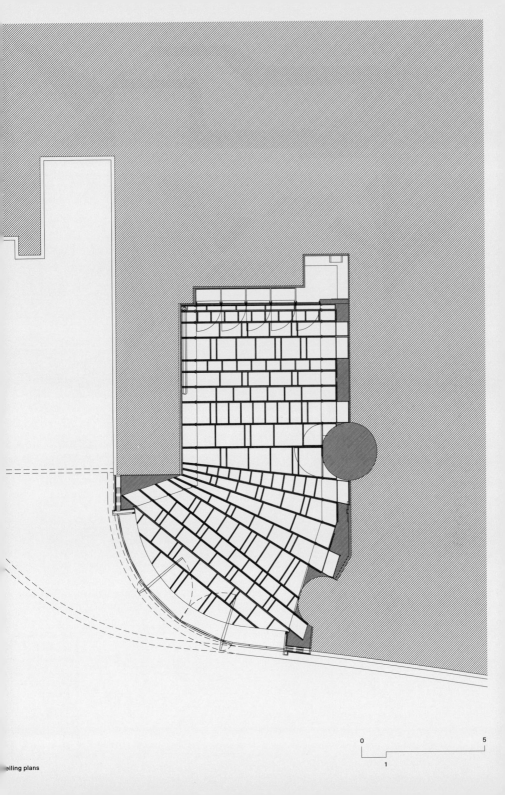

0   5

1

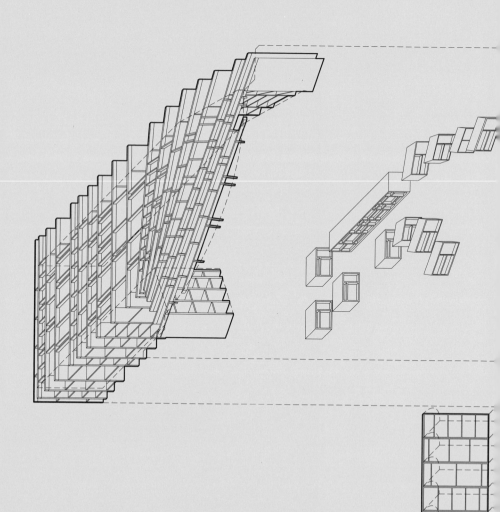

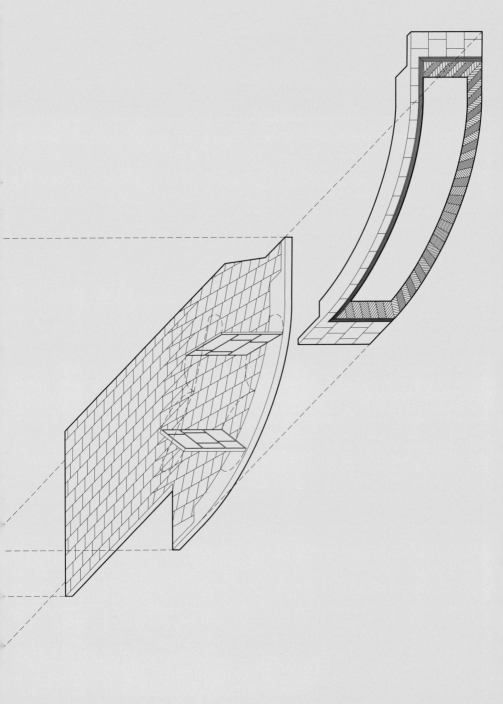

loded oblique

0   5

1

tail Wall Section

Stainless Steel
LED Spotlight
Slimline light fitting
20mm Plywood Support,
Set in 50mm on both sides
Stainless Steel Recess
for Adjustable Shelf
20mm thick Marine Grade
Plywood
Solid Core High Gloss Laminate
Demising Wall

Shelf Elevation

1   Stainless Steel
2   Removable Glass Display Case
3   Tapered Recess
4   Homogeneous Sill Limestone
    Tile on Mortar

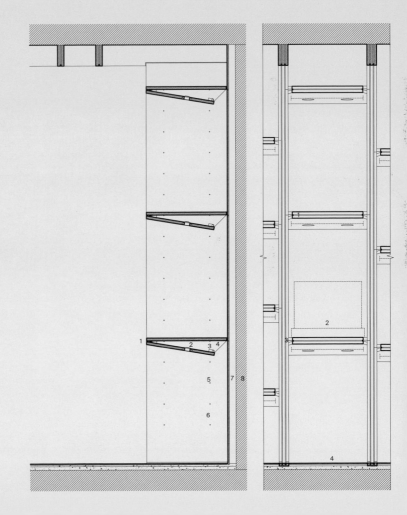

Exploded oblique

0   5

1

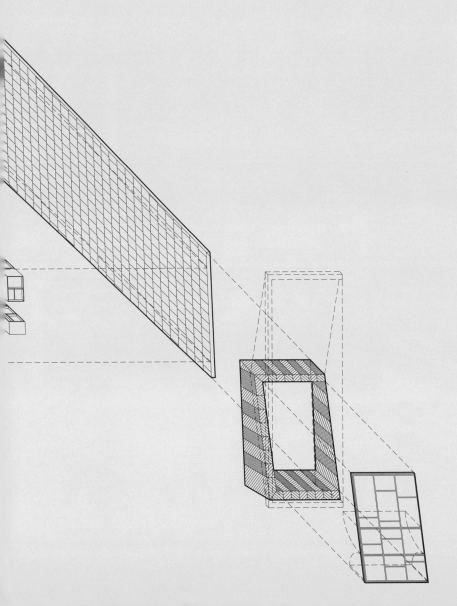

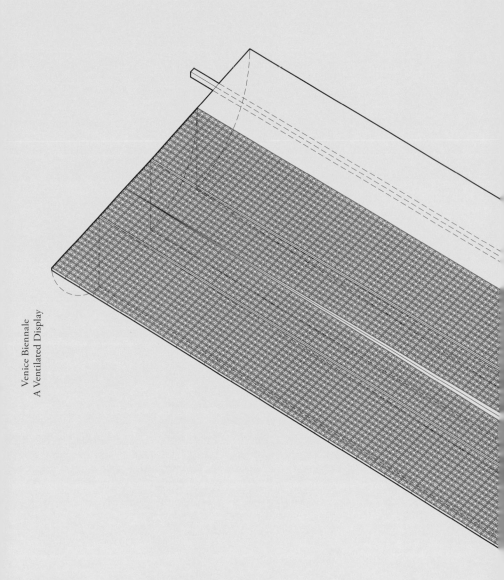

Venice Biennale
A Ventilated Display

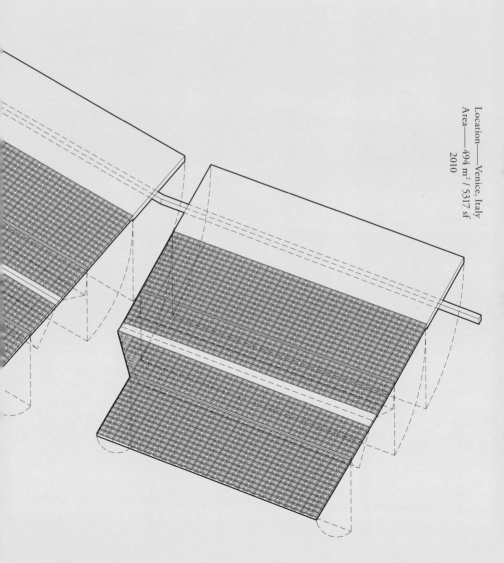

Location——Venice, Italy
Area——494 m² / 5317 sf
2010

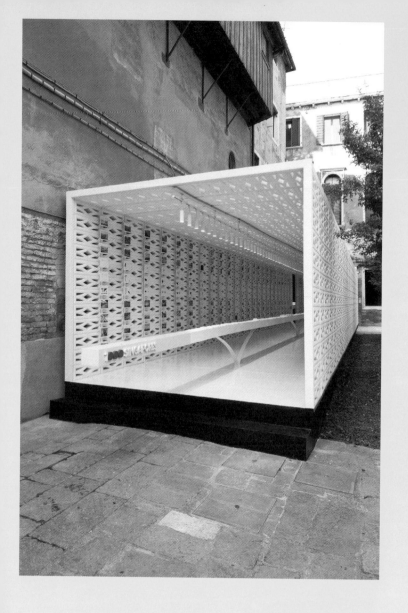

Venice Biennale
A Ventilated Display

*What kind of experience can be offered by the veil—optical,
phenomenological, intellectual?*

The exhibition *1,000 Singapores: A Model of the Compact City* was
designed and built for the Singapore National Pavilion at the 2010
Venice Biennale. The architecture was composed of two strategies with
different scale—macro and micro. At the macro scale, a 30-meter-long
trellis tube was positioned between an exterior courtyard and an interior
gallery on the ground floor of the Istituto Provinciale per l'Infanzia. The
tube wrapped a 35-meter-long "Singapore sample" in the form of a long,
intricate model—a slice of the nation state. Rendered in white ABS
plastic, the slice of Singapore formed the primary spine of the exhibition.

 The tube was extruded between two end profiles, one rectilinear in
shape and alluding to the public housing that accommodates 83% of
the nation's resident population, and the other taking the recognizable
pitched-roof outline of the residential house. In addition to housing the
exhibition content, the long tube also served as the only means of access
into the interior galleries. The exterior end profile framed a view of one
of Venice's canals, bringing Singapore and Venice into visual proximity.
The tube was bifurcated where it met the entrance to Istituto
Provinciale—the very location where Vivaldi composed *Le Quattro
Stagioni (The Four Seasons)*. A wedge was subtracted from the tube at this
threshold, allowing for expanded circulation while marking a kink in
the plan. The design was purposely neither fully exterior nor entirely
interior; rather, it has the both exterior and interior qualities. Likewise,
the design oscillated between being read as a temporary installation and
a permanent spatial extension of the original historic architecture.

At the micro scale, a series of metal frames ran the length of the tube forming its primary structure. Positioned between them were a series of EIFS polystyrene ventilation blocks placed in a stack-bond configuration. An allusion to the tropical screens of Southeast Asia, the blocks produced an elongated veil, screening the exhibition proper. Light and air were permitted through, but views were obstructed. The veil, rendered in white stucco, was calibrated to the crisp Venice sun creating a subtle atmosphere of even natural lighting, gentle breeze, and dampened acoustics. The architectural effect was a gallery-like setting where contemplation of the exhibition content was the priority.

Within, 1,000 postcards were positioned around 6 inches (150 millimeters) proud of the screen. As such, focus was set off the elevations and the architecture could be perceived as a background—experienced in an unfocused state. Simultaneously, fragmented views could be seen through the blocks. Resultingly, the optical performance of the veil drove the phenomenological and experiential qualities of the design. The architecture was fabricated in Singapore and shipped to Venice for installation. Weight, structural loading, and the logistics of transportation through the canals of Venice all drove a design subtext: a deployable modular system. At the exhibition's close, the entire exhibition and architecture were repackaged and returned to Singapore in wait for its next deployment.

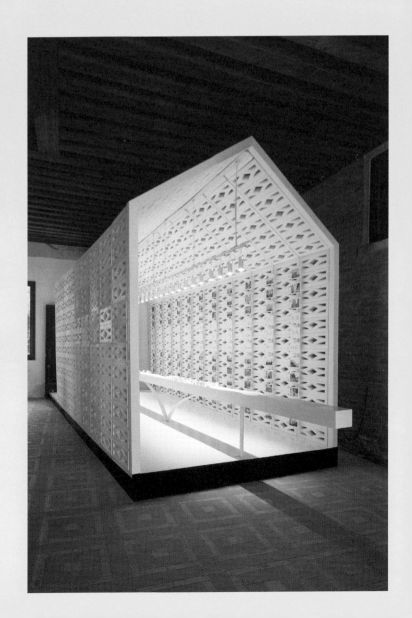

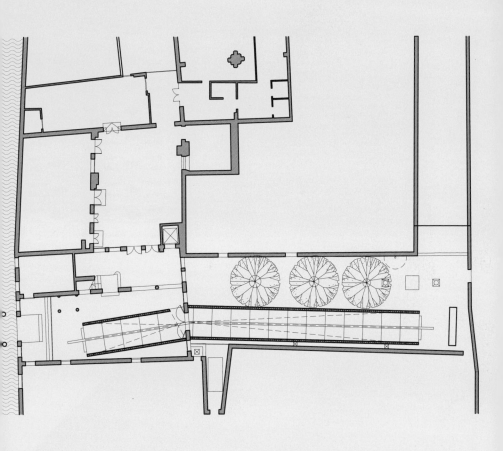

1000 SINGAPORES

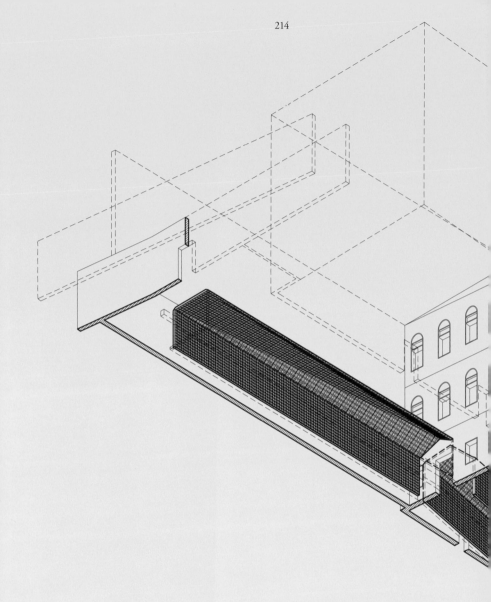

0   10

Worm's eye sectional axonometric   1

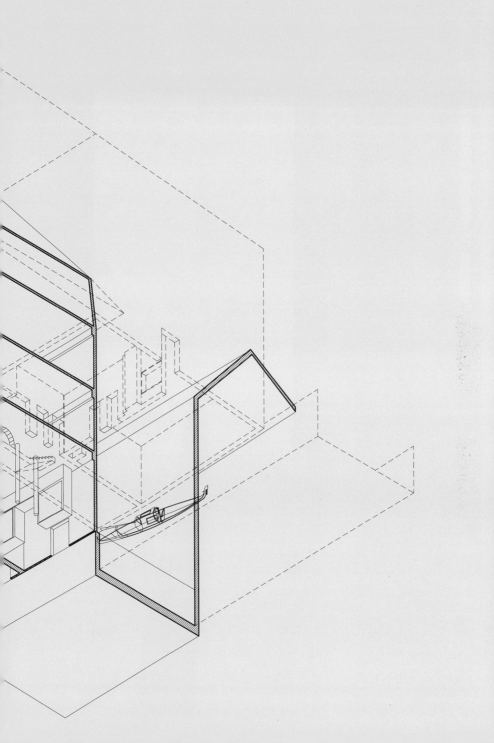

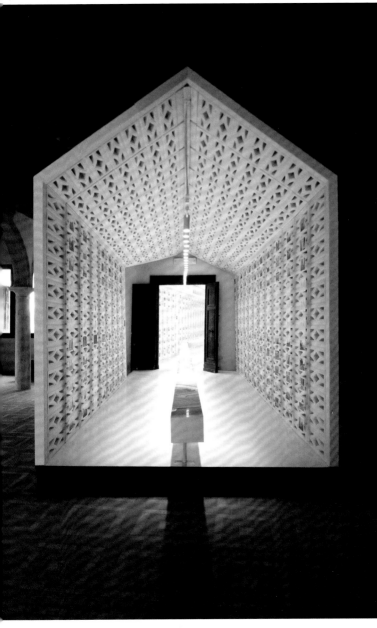

A Simple Brick Interior

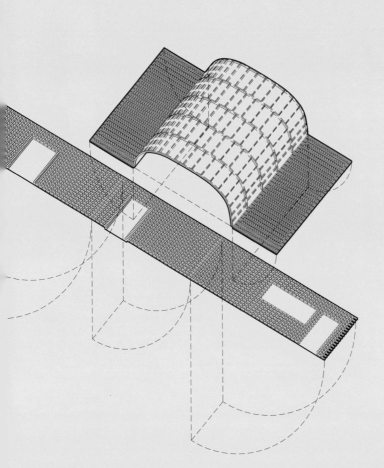

Location——Phoenix Park, Singapore

Area——193 m² / 2077 sf

2012

A Simple Brick Interior

On how many levels can a veil perform? How can the material with which a veil is constructed be choreographed for delightful visual effects?

A simple, but dramatic, interior wrapper of white-painted brick surrounds the vertical surfaces of the main dining room of Commune—a 1,539-square-foot (143-square-metre) restaurant designed and built in 2012. Located in the Tanglin area of Singapore, in the historic Phoenix Park compound (once a British military outpost), the design purposefully interferes with and obscures views to the exterior landscape. This is a means of blocking unsightly views while allowing breeze and light into the interior. The continuous perforated screen composed of standard solid bricks alternates about each coursing, rotated perpendicular to the row below and above.

The simple, repeatable element is made consistent except for one variable: the perpendicular brick pattern subtly undulates in plan, moving in and out to accommodate existing columns, openings, and air conditioning components. The effect is a subtle gradation, producing a dynamic experience of movement similar to that found in the paintings and sculptures of artists exploring optical effects. Works by Bridget Riley, Julio Le Parc, and Victor Vasarely are examples. The resulting optical effect recalls the ventilation screens of mid-century tropical ventilation architecture. At night, the optical obfuscation is inverted, and the restaurant takes on the appearance of a glowing lantern, emitting light to the exterior.

The graphic identity of the restaurant is inlaid on the concrete floor as well as table tops—small details that produce a cohesive design experience. The other surfaces (floor, ceiling, kitchen walls) are purposefully subdued in terms of visual impact. This is a reductive design strategy to focus and maximize the impact of the perforated brick screen.

A Simple Brick Interior illustrates how the most straightforward of materials—bricks—when carefully and thoughtfully deployed, can produce comfort and excitement, screen and effect, wall and veil in a design of simple, yet powerful elegance.

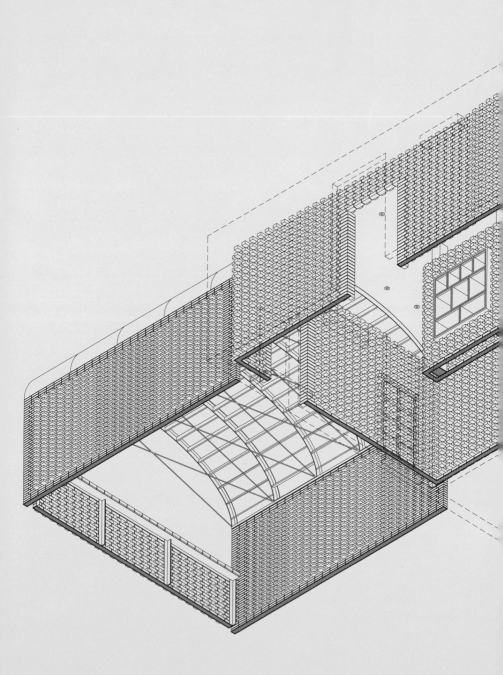

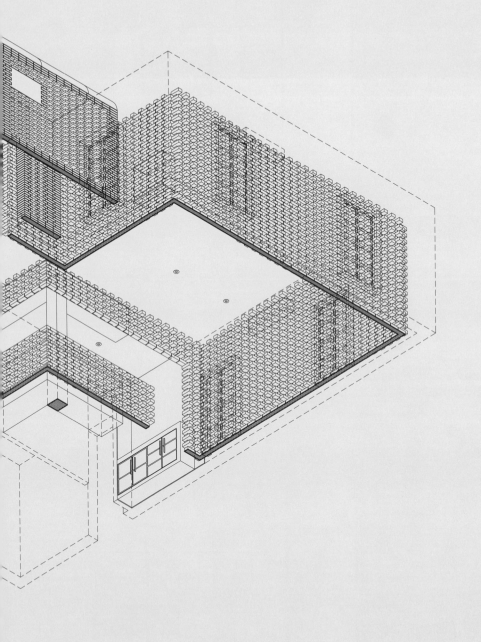

worm's eye sectional axonometric

0   1   5

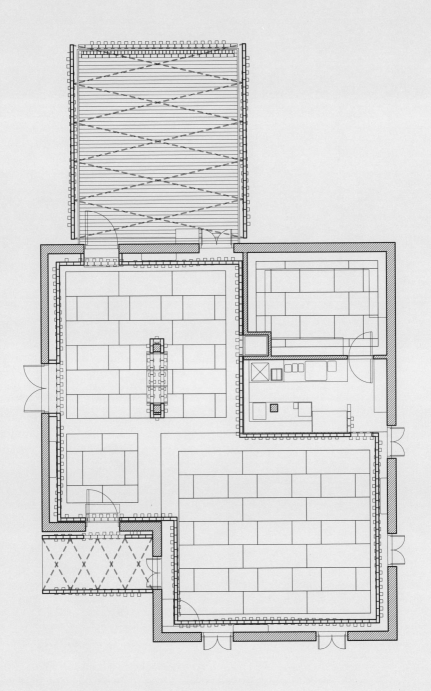

0   5

1

n

ail Wall Section

Metal channel
Concrete floor
Brick wall
Ceiling plenum
Timber window frame
Perimetral drain

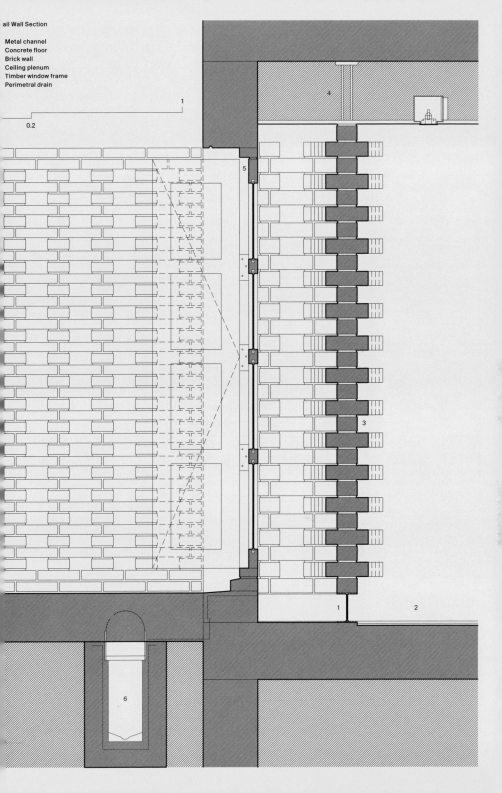

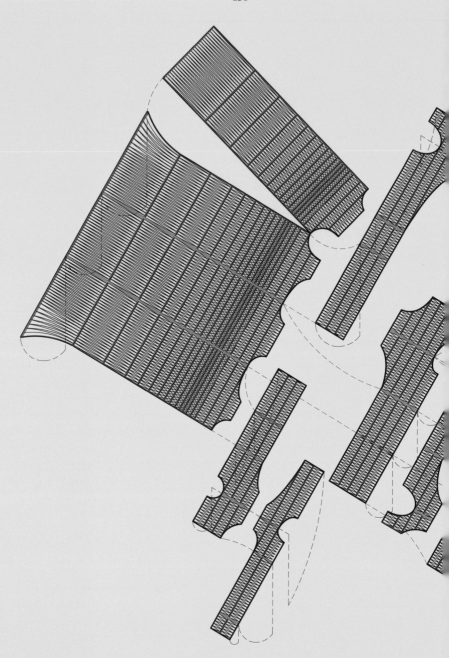

Neighborhood Towers

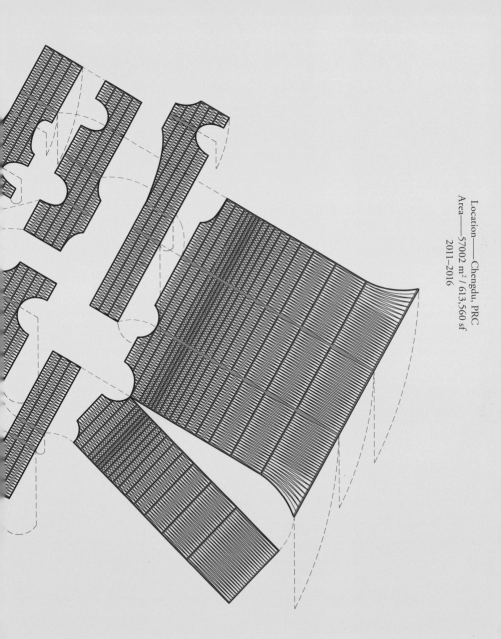

Location——Chengdu, PRC
Area——57002 m² / 613,560 sf
2011–2016

Neighborhood Towers

What can the veil achieve as an urban element? What structural work can the veil undertake?

Situated in the Jin Nui district of Chengdu, China, the 538,200-square-foot (50,000-square-meter) Neighborhood Towers was designed between 2011 and 2012. Two urban architectural questions are addressed as the basis of the design's formation. Firstly, how can architecture mitigate the problems of the existing master plan while amplifying the successful public life adjacent to the immediate site? Secondly, how can the architecture create a new relationship between the institutions of the Chengdu Government Service Center as its primary program while encouraging a closer, more intimate relationship between citizens and government?

The design strategy proposes a counter-narrative to the approved master plan that is currently reshaping the district. Podium block profiles dominate the current master plan. Though they would accommodate the larger building scale required by massive urbanization, the consequence of the master plan is the obliteration of successful, productive, and socially coherent neighborhoods. The Neighborhood Towers design engages in this reality by forming a series of smaller-scale interconnected volumes at the podium level. Each volume has a different footprint and dimensional proportion. This variety accommodates a mix of programs at the pedestrian street level, while allowing for cohesive and continuous space for the public service center to exist side by side.

The volumes at the street level are separated by pedestrian-scaled alleyways and courtyards of various sizes, which extend the existing neighborhood networks into the site proper. Small-scale businesses, learning centers, and retail are encouraged at lower levels, while the functions of the citizens' service center are positioned above. This strategy embraces maximum envelope and public frontage as a powerful urban strategy. This runs counter to the monolithic podium volumes with vast interiors typified by much development today.

The close proximity of public and private space along the frontage encourages the mingling of a diverse mix of people who will occupy the site throughout the day and night. In this case, public space and public institutions immediately impact the city at large, reaffirming public city life as an aspiration of Chengdu. Curvilinear subtractions at the corners of each of the volumes create sheltered pubic spaces and internally positioned courtyards that are open to the public. Two larger towers emerge out of this aggregation of small volumes, providing the speculative real estate demanded by the unique public-private interrelated financial basis of the project.

Architecturally, an anamorphic projected trellis veil wraps each of the volumes while amplifying the overcast natural light found in Chengdu deep into the interior spaces. The subtly shifting density in the trellis pattern creates the illusion of a much taller structure, drawing the eyes vertically toward the sky. Coated in photocatalytic titanium dioxide, the veil is self-cleaning and assists in substantially reducing concentrations of airborne pollutants in the immediate area. The curtain wall behind the trellis is of a highly reflective silver coating, optically mirroring the trellis. The optical qualities of the trellis are subverted by its own doubling, rendering the screening as optical interference and effect. Analogous to the experiments of the optical artists in the 1960s, the screen's design entails the deployment of a simple form to create a shimmering, disquieting effect.

In this case, the façade also performs structurally, bearing all of the perimeter loads and allowing column-free floor plates. Grey bricks, found throughout Chengdu, will be deployed on all of the curving surfaces, merging streets and pockets of public space in a continuous material surface. The bricks, a material commonly used in local practice

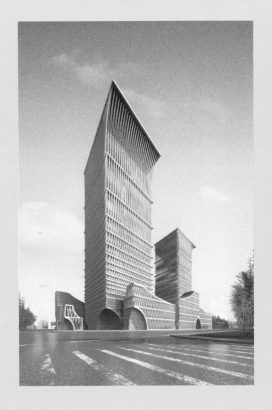

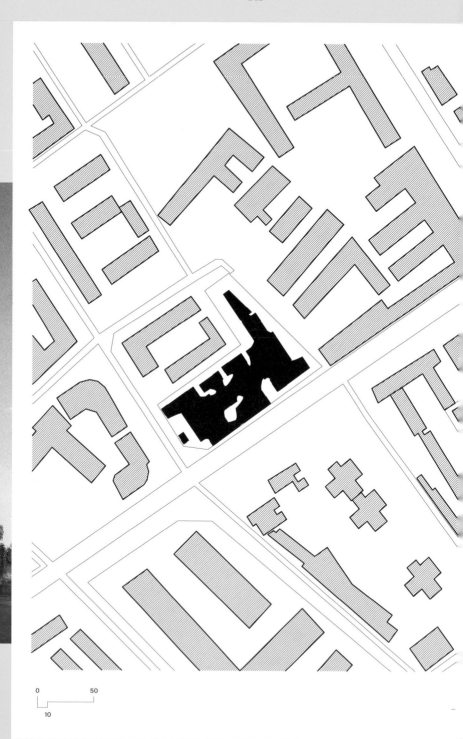

0   50
10

as evident in many historical buildings in Chengdu, are now used strategically in a novel curvilinear configuration and deployed at a larger scale. The roof forms follow a similar geometry and material composition, merging the variety of spaces into a cohesive whole. At the urban, programmatic, and architectural levels, the project's ambition is to engage in the realities of a city rapidly urbanizing and searching for its own identity, while amplifying and extending its own very successes as the basis for the design strategy.

8th floor

N   0   50

10

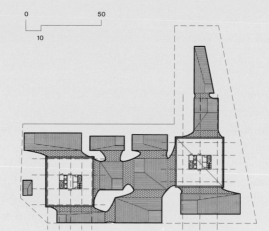

4th floor

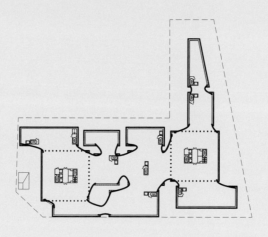

Ground floor

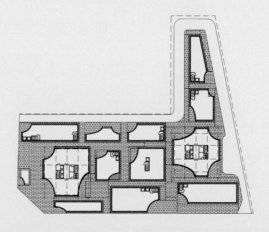

ail Wall Section

Mechanical Plenum with
12mm GYP Ceiling
Operable Awning Units
Low E Duble Glazed
Insulated Unit
RC Structural Rise Solid
Column with Stucco
10x50x100mm SS Balustrade
RC Waffle Slab
Operable Roller Curtain
50mm Rigid Insulation
Precast Sub-frame
Chengdu Grey Brick,
Running Course

0   1

0.2

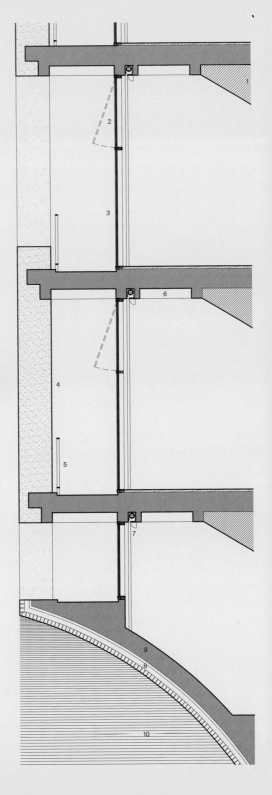

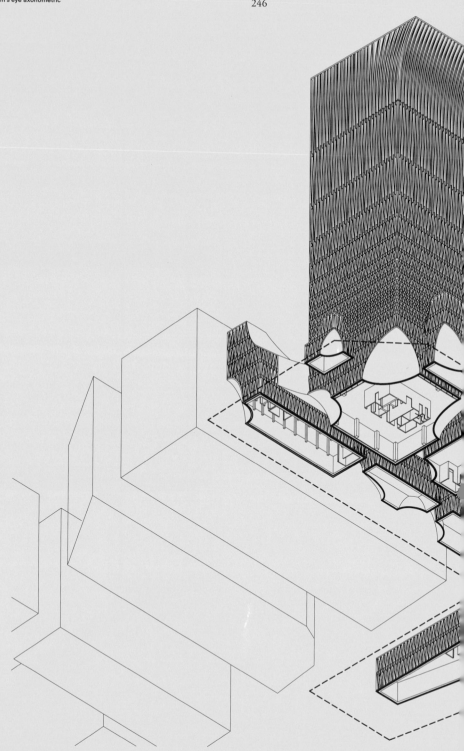

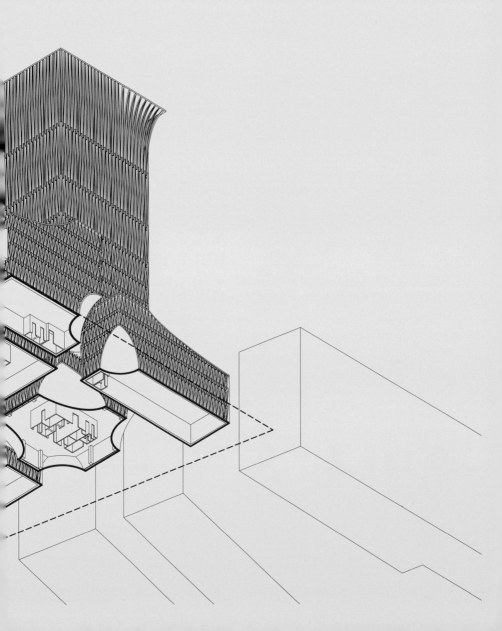

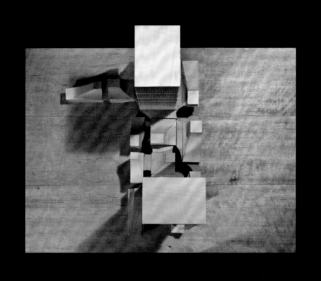

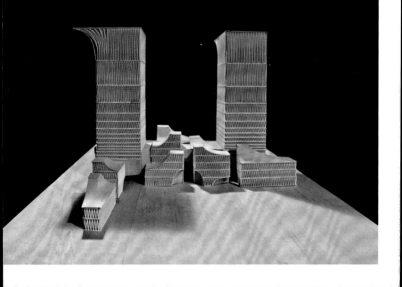

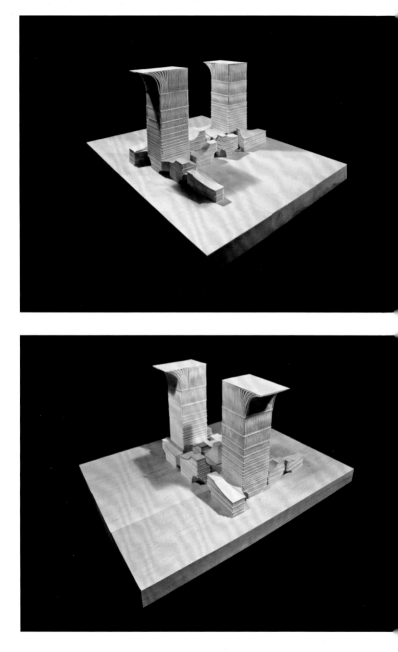

0   50
10

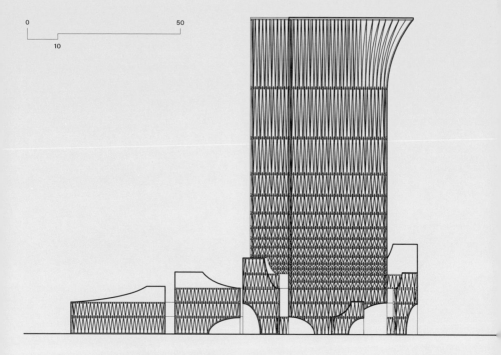

South elevation

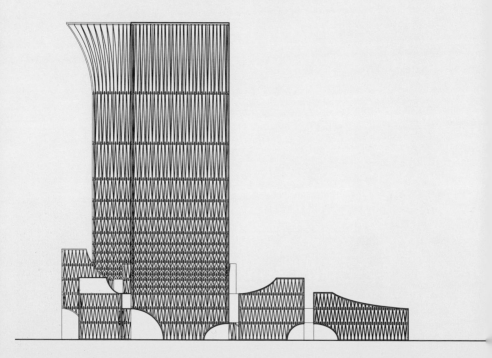

North elevation

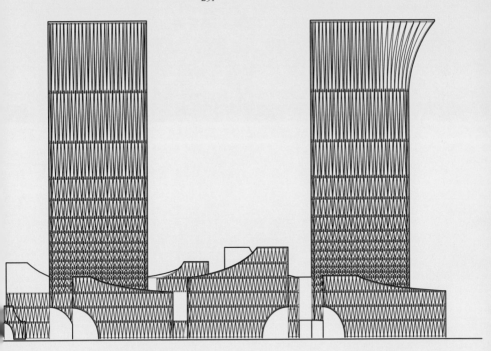

st elevation

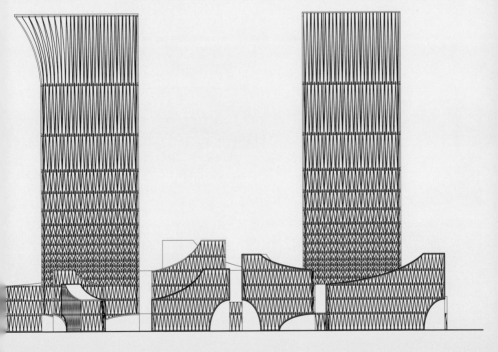

st elevation

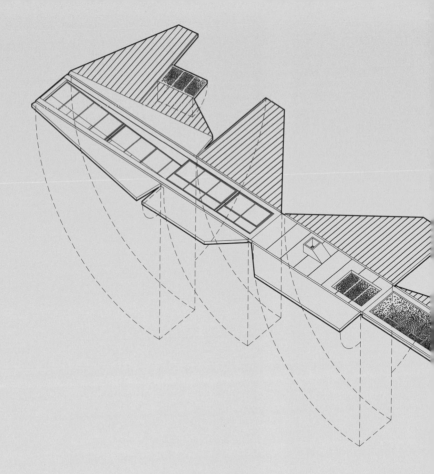

Pile Houses

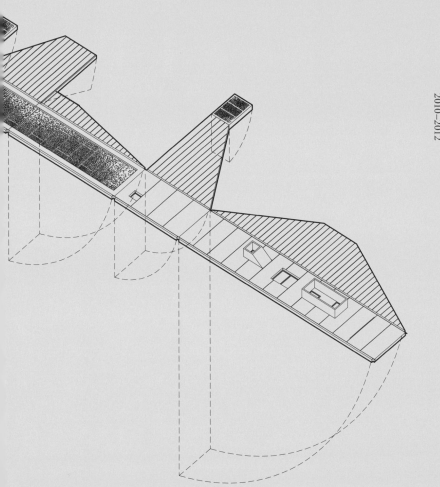

Location———Johor Bahru, Malaysia
Area individual unit———526 m² / 5670 sf
Area 26 units———45,161 m² / 486,109 sf
2010–2012

Pile Houses

How can the veil mediate one's relationship with their neighborhood? En masse, can it create a neighborhood?

An existing pile grid located in a cul-de sac between two golf courses in Johor Bahru, Malaysia forms the foundation of the project. Originally piled in 1995, the site was abandoned after the 1997 Asian financial crisis. Between 2010 and 2013, after 13 years of dereliction, the new architecture was tasked with resurrecting the ambitions of earlier years. The design extends the original pile grid into 26 new houses, transforming a generic housing development into a small neighborhood of cohesiveness, environmental concern, and optical calibration. One house has been constructed to date.

Three agendas drove the design. The primary ambition was to utilize the existing pile grid and structures on site, conserving existing resources, limiting structural reworking, and taking advantage of what exists in the formation of the new architecture. The second ambition was to strategically modify the urban configuration of the road and cul-de sac to amplify the neighborhood, minimize the hardscape, and maximize public green space throughout the development. The final ambition was to make visible the operations of real estate speculation through an amplification—albeit a critical one—of "the view".

Architecturally, the houses will take six different configurations based on the pile locations. "L", "U", "O", "Bar", and "Block" shapes form the basic plan configurations, all with different sizes and orientations. Each house will range from 3,500 to 7,500 square feet (325 to 696 square meters) in size. The designs will accommodate three generations of family—up to twelve people. Six original house structures were retained, though modified for the new architectural configurations, updated, and repurposed.

When all are constructed, the houses will share a large entry courtyard that flanks the main street. The intent of the courtyard is to resist the complete privatization of the neighborhood, as is typical in Southeast Asian developments, while providing an increased planting belt accessible to the public. In effect, the courtyard incorporates boundary walls, security features, and an internalized private outdoor space. Rendered in a grey homogeneous tile sourced in Malaysia, the walls unify the neighborhood spatially and materially while creating a relatively opaque and fortified frontage. The opaque frontage also functions as a physical barrier, amplifying the security concerns of buyers in this region while obscuring and directing views of the golf course beyond. The second storeys are planometrically displaced from the first storey configuration, cantilevering in some areas to produce shaded overhangs beneath.

Seen in longitudinal elevation, the first house is suggestive of an optical machine that both conceals and reveals. As approached from the street, the house is (in a manner similar to the Stereoscopic House) signified by a pitched roof which, in this case, is an aggregation of three. A frontal façade composed of operable panels (cut by water jet) obscures the house and its internal program while minimizing thermal heat gain from the western sun. In essence, the frontal façade of the house is purposefully rendered opaque—a solid mass facing the street. The pattern on the aluminum panels has been applied as a gradient with more perforations at areas offering views, and less perforations where privacy is required.

The elevation facing the golf course has been calibrated for an entirely different end. A deepened envelope of overhangs and verandahs constructs a more dynamic elevation in deep relief. Large expanses of operable glass open to create an expansive view of the golf course beyond. A large roof protrusion pops up uncomfortably from the center of the elevation, set over the living room proper, thrusting the gaze upwards. Rather than connoting "house", the roof protrusion signifies and performs as a volumetric expansion of the interior spaces, and as a thermal chimney. The side elevations are primarily opaque, focusing the gaze to the golf course, specifically to the eighteenth hole.

Subtle, yet important, updates to the original planning of the cul-de sac enhance what would otherwise be a generic development. The road width is reduced and sidewalks are flanked by large planting areas. Each of the plot areas has been repurposed to contribute to the street landscape, with part of each property in effect donated for the enjoyment of the wider neighborhood. Seen as a collective, the architectural forms generate two distinct spaces and spatial experiences: an entirely private and protected courtyard forming the communal entry space for each house, and a typology of aggregated roof forms that, through a common architectural trope, produce a collective identity necessary for the scale of the neighborhood. Combined with the optical effects of looking out onto the landscape, as a series of optical lenses, the pile houses embrace and expose the primary modes of development in Southeast Asia.

This approach to roof design will be consistent across all of the houses. The aggregate roof landscape will also serve to modulate the scale of the neighborhood into smaller components, breaking up the normative articulation of roof to plot. The tapered forms will also extend vertically within each of the houses, bringing in filtered natural light from above and allowing heated air from the interior to be evacuated. Rendered in a deep brown with iron oxide pigment, the finishing will allow the dramatic quality of the architecture to be seen in its totality as a neighborhood, rather than in terms of the overt individualism that is common in similarly scaled developments in the region.

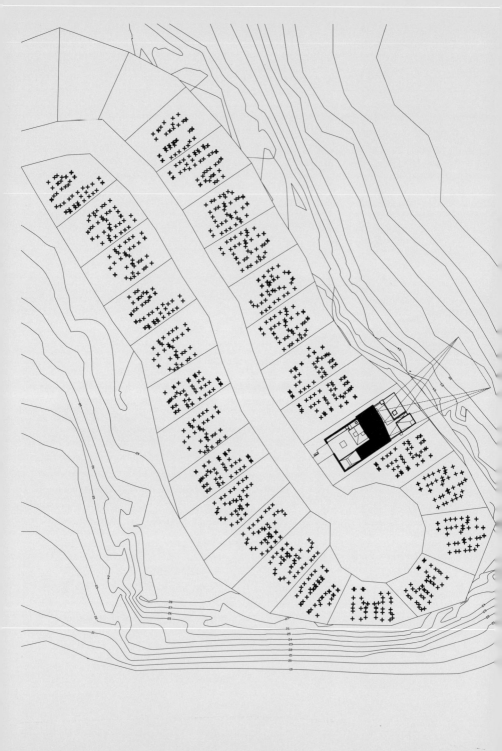

Pile plan

ghborhood plan

N

0   100

10

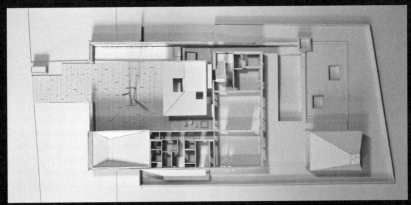

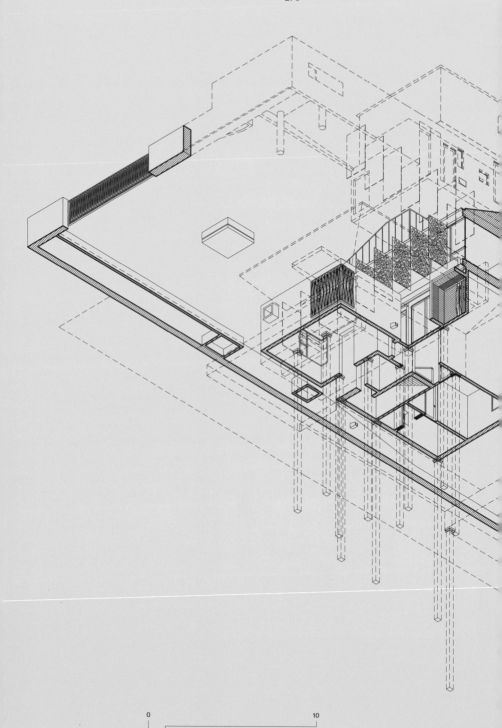

Worm's eye sectional axonometric

0   10

1

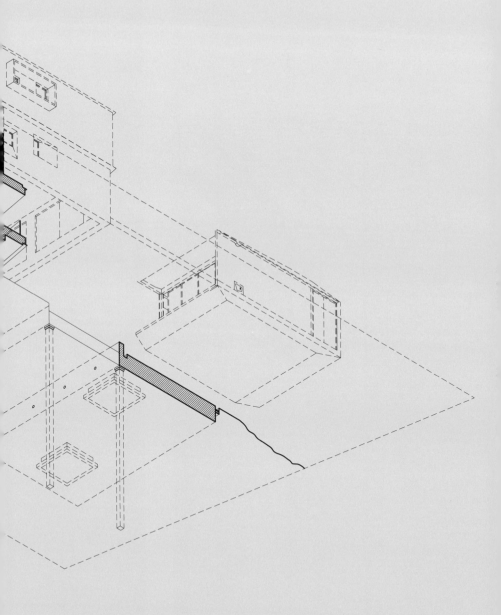

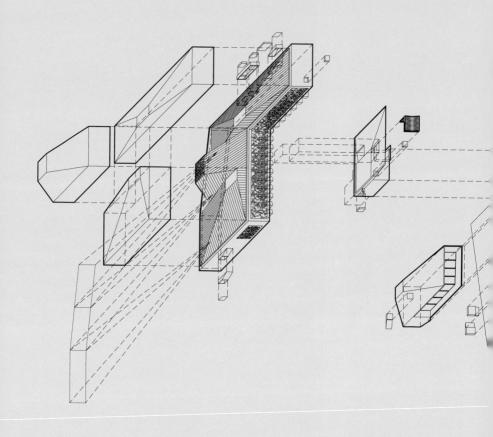

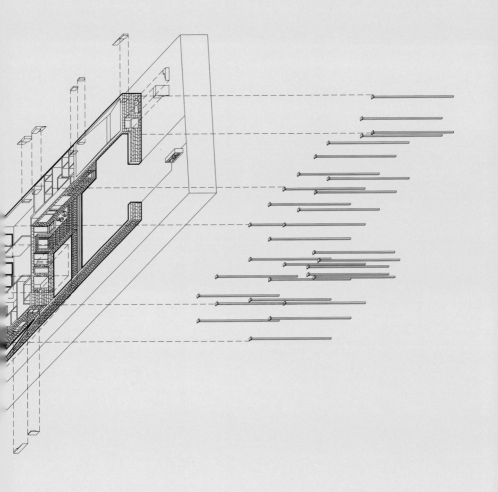

oded oblique

0   10

1

West elevation

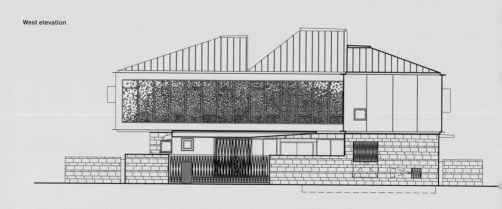

North elevation

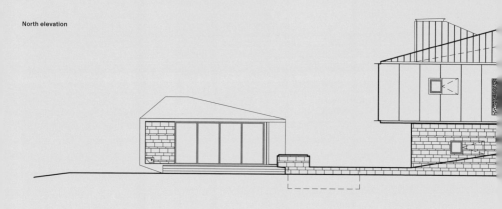

Longitudinal elevation

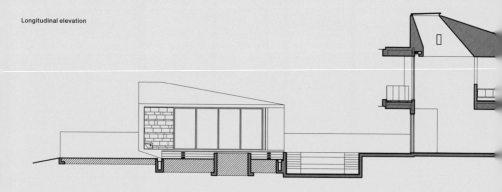

ss section

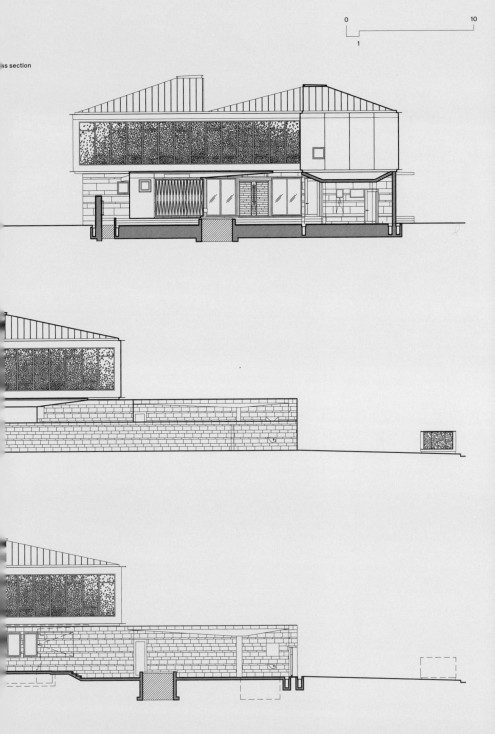

0
1
10

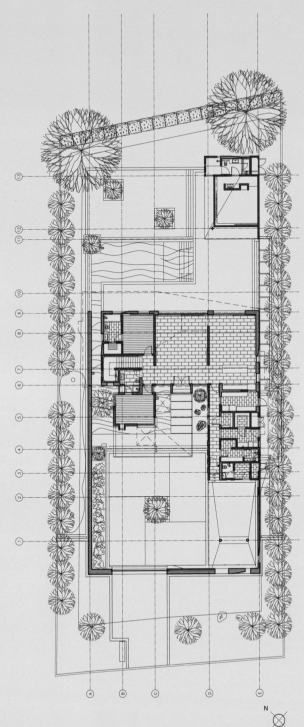

N

0   10
1

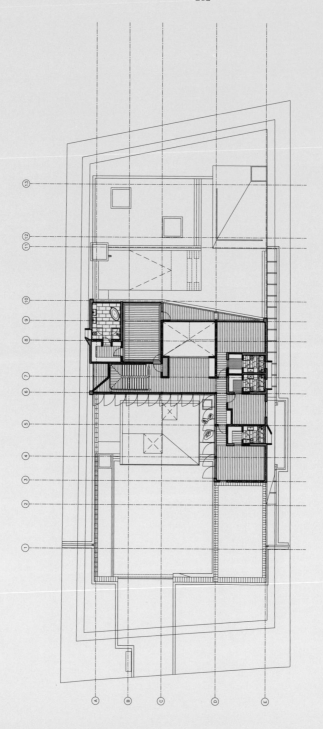

2nd floor

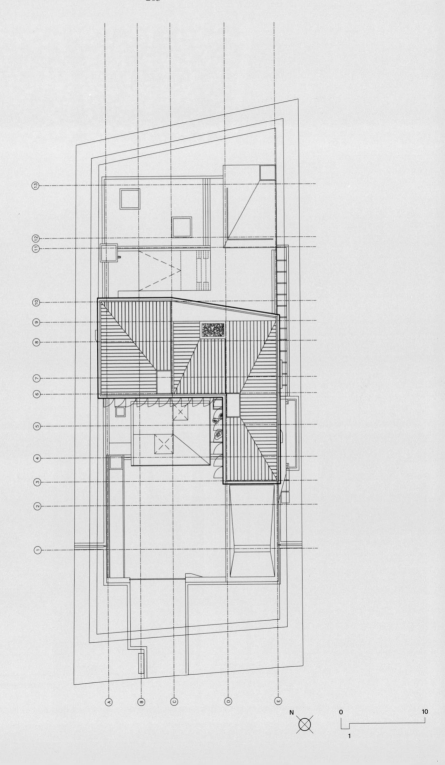

plan

N

0   10

1

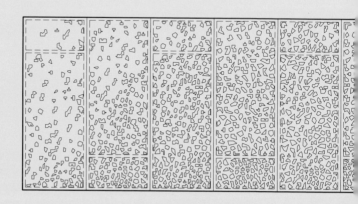

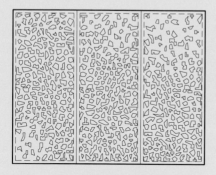

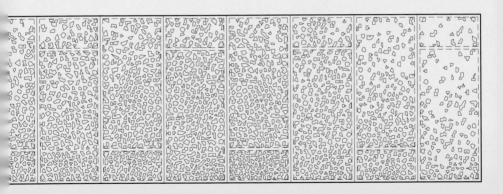

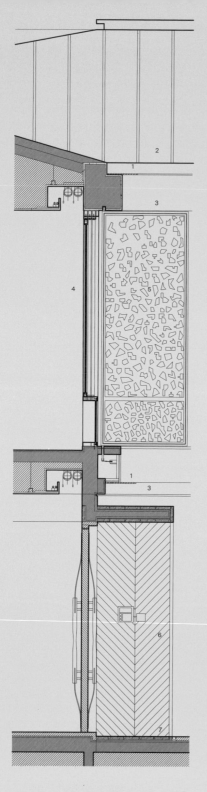

Detail Wall Section

1 Drip edge, 5x250mm
   galvinized metal
2 Metal standing seam roof
3 Iron oxide stucco finish
4 Low E aluminum sliding windo
5 Water jet cut operable
   aluminum screen
6 25mm teak, herringbone
   threshold
7 Homogeneous granite pavers

0

0.2

A Simple Factory Building

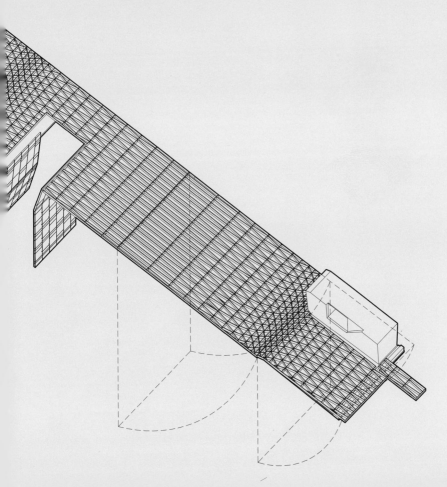

Location———Singapore
Area———991.8 m² / 10,676 sf
2009–2012

A Simple
Factory Building

Can the veil reconcile conflicting demands? Can it interfere with the perception of normative architectural form? Can it redefine a common architectural typology?

A Simple Factory Building addresses two contradicting demands: the mitigation of tropical solar radiation, and the openness to view sought by the clients in a basic industrial typology. Designed and built between 2009 and 2012, the 10,742-square-foot (998-square-meter) building is located in an industrial area of Singapore. It utilizes a sophisticated 4-foot-deep (1.2-meter-deep) veil fabricated in lightweight Dryvit and a bronze full-height window-wall envelope to reconcile this architectural conflict.

Wrapping continuously as a loop around the front elevation, car porch ceiling, rear elevation, and roof, the veil shields the building from the harsh tropical sunlight while calibrating views to the exterior. It also amplifies natural illumination, directs natural ventilation, and conceals mechanical equipment. It calibrates the performance of the building as a climatic engine.

In addition to shading the building from direct sunlight, the veil's pattern changes to views to the neighboring park while obstructing unsightly views to the immediate vicinity of the industrial neighborhood. The degree of perforation varies to create openness and privacy in relation to internal programming. From street level, the resulting façade is seen as an anamorphic pattern that creates an optical disturbance to the normative clues that describe the scale of buildings and allow for floor counts. This interference is purposeful; it calibrates the building as an optical device for the performance of inhabitation within and reading from without. Likewise, the normative architectural categories of façade, roof, and ceiling, are upset by the continuous wrapping of the veil; the distinct architectural categories are merged into one continuous deep envelope.

A Simple Factory Building was conceived as a block of four double-height levels—in essence, an eight-storey building. A volumetric subtraction from its center creates an open courtyard that maximizes natural lighting and ventilation to the building's interior. Three small balconies extend into this central void, alluding to the frontal balcony of Villa Stein, but allowing a view only to the sky above. Six-meter floor-to-floor interior heights ensure warm air rises above the workspaces. A large opening in the eastern party wall (profiling the courtyard's section) allows the only uninterrupted view from the interior to the exterior, directing the gaze toward clusters of tropical tree canopies. However, the bronze reflective glass surrounding the courtyard mirrors alternate exterior scenes creating a kaleidoscopic effect; thus even here the unobstructed view is contaminated with dramatic reflections.

A service core stretches the length of the building along its western façade and performs as a thermal mass, buffering the habitable workspaces beyond and ensuring minimal thermal gain to the interior. Raised off the ground, the building mass maximizes cross ventilation as a means to cool the interior. The reflective bronze aluminum window walls, simple reinforced construction, and minimal use of petroleum membranes mean that the building will be almost entirely recyclable when the site is redeveloped in the near future—a typical occurrence in the Singapore context of perpetual tabula rasa.

The veil of A Simple Factory Building is anything but simple. Complex geometries and intersecting profiles were made possible through CNC routing and computer-controlled hot wire cutting. Though alluding to screening devices found throughout Southeast Asia, the veil performs myriad roles, merging atmospheric, performance, and inhabitation practices into one. As a screening device, A Simple Factory Building's veil is an apt counter-narrative to the temperate region's

0 200
50

fascination with glass and transparency. Both closed and open, both shadowed and reflective, both permitting view and creating interference, the project illustrates that architecture can be a robust and powerful undertaking, even for banal industrial typologies.

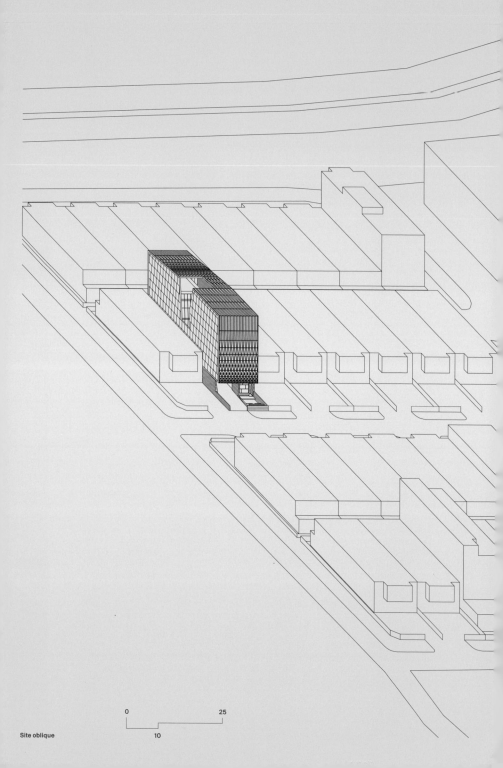

Site oblique

0   25
10

East elevation

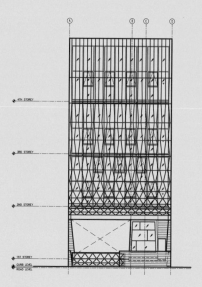

West elevation

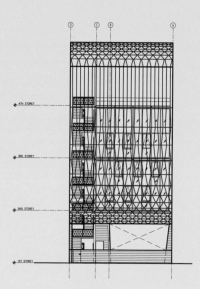

south elevation

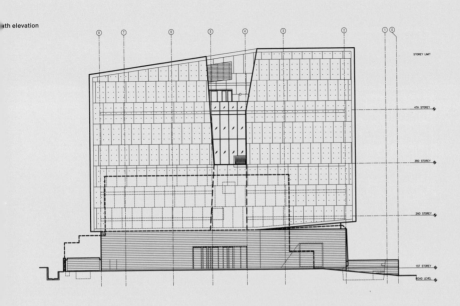

longitudinal section

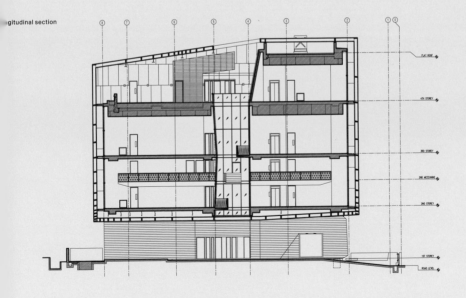

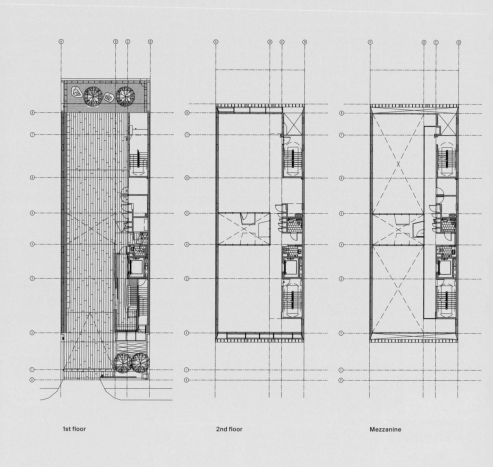

1st floor   2nd floor   Mezzanine

0   10

1

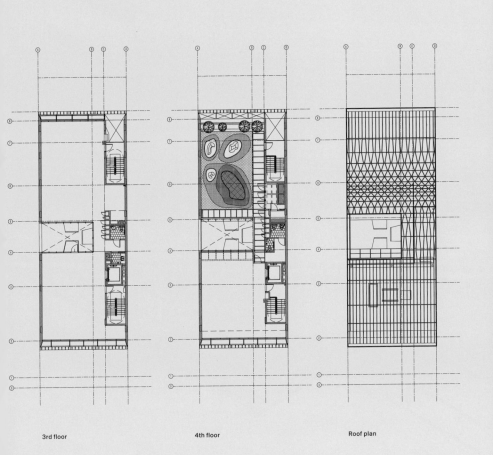

3rd floor

4th floor

Roof plan

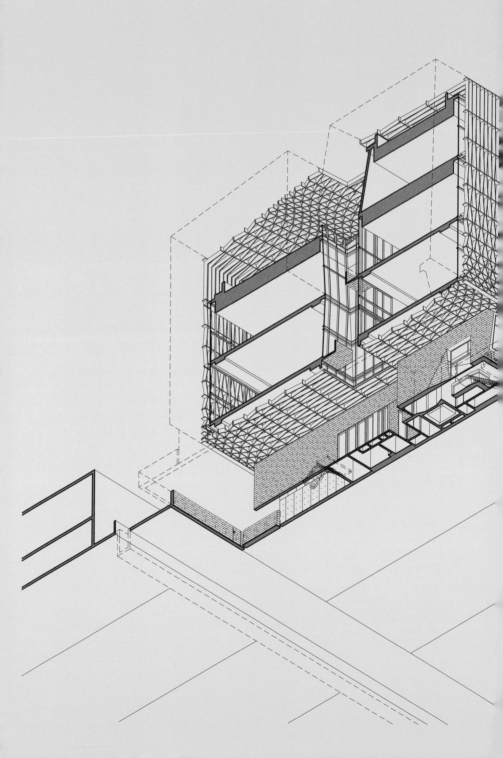

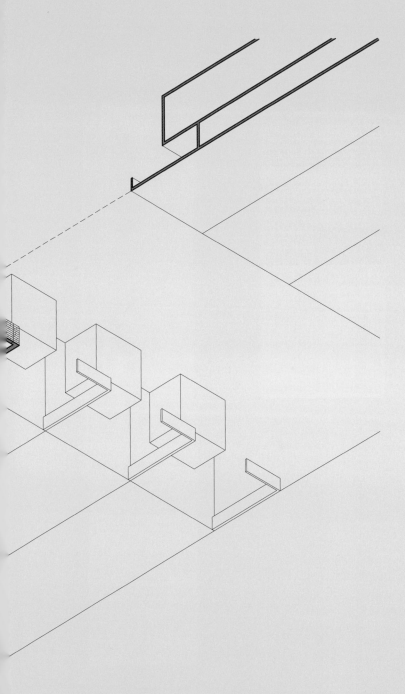

n's eye sectional axonometric

tail Wall Section

Galvanized metal
hollow section frame
EIFS CNC cut panel
Fair-face concrete pattern wall
Top hung aluminium window,
bronze laminate glazing
LED light fixture
50x50mm galvanized metal
hollow section
50x50mm metal angle
Internal metal sub frame
8x80x160mm galvanized
metal tube
300x90mm galvanized metal
parallel flange
LED light fixture
Board form concrete wall
assembly

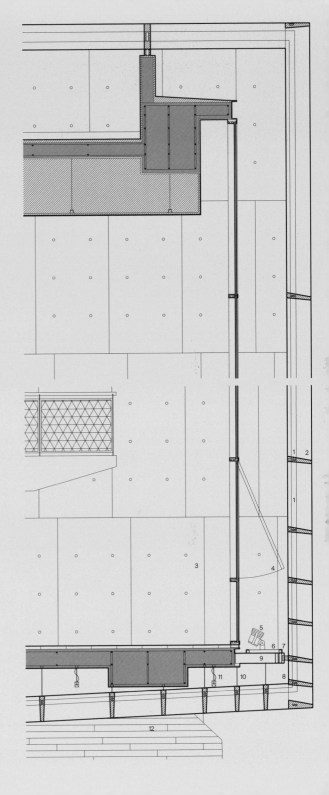

1

0.2

Environmental section

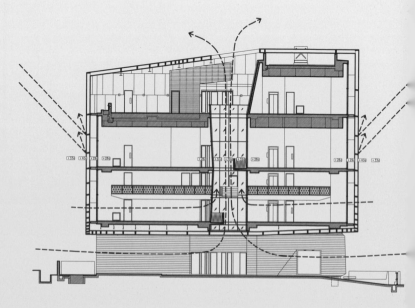

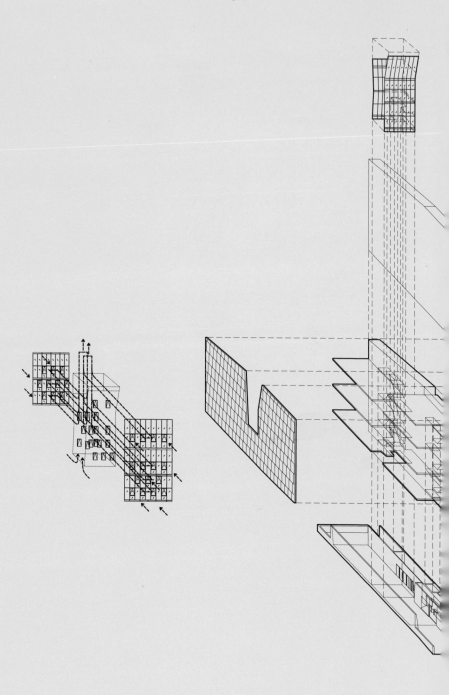

Exploded oblique

0

20

2

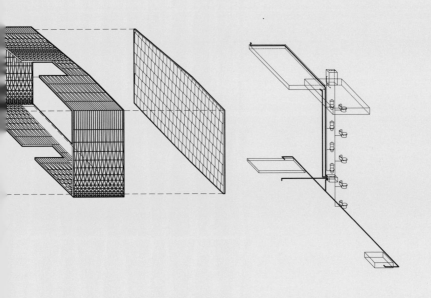

Unveiling Veil

In the architecture of Erik L'Heureux, there is an exploration of the unification spatially and structurally, the unification of covering and binding.

In terms selected by Erik L'Heureux: the veil, to veil, we find the clue to understanding the beauty behind the veil, and our task is to unveil, unveiling the veil.

The veil unveiling is a discourse on the act of construction, on the idea made into a built reality to form an experience, a consequent elevation of discourse to a higher degree, the surface and structure, unified and made into one, or rather unmade two into one, towards the production of effects and corresponding psychological, sociological, and physical effects.

Two quotes to guide our thoughts:

One taken from Erik L'Heureux's *Deep Veils*:
'Architecture is the production of experience built from drawings and ideas made into space and material.'

and the other one taken from Gottfried Semper's *Style in the Technical and Tectonic Arts; or, Practical Aesthetics* (1860):
'The essence of architecture is its covering layer rather than its material structure.'

These two quotes bring us to the essential idea that unveiling the veil is an operation on thinking and re-thinking, how we build.

How do we wrap a veil and unveil it around ourselves? An eternal discussion in the construction of architecture, the pursuit of an intelligent approach to making spaces to house the emotional realm.

A discourse where the old lives and complimented by the new, a discourse where the landscape, structure, and space are integrated and form a unified whole, an operation that is fundamental, and erotic.

Erwin Viray
Professor and Head
Graduate School of Architecture Design at
Kyoto Institute of Technology, Japan

Acknowledgements

Architecture is not different from a musical ensemble. In an ensemble, the composer, the conductor, and musicians all perform together to create a harmonious melody. In this symphony called architecture, the members of the orchestra include the consultants, the local Architects of Record, the craftsmen, as well as others whose contributions have enabled the realization of this small body of work. To them, I am deeply grateful. I would like to take this opportunity to acknowledge those who have contributed to works in these pages. Should there be any names I inadvertently left out, I apologize in advance.

To my colleagues at the National University of Singapore who challenge, inspire, and occasionally frustrate—all for the better—, I am greatly indebted. Their support and intellectual presence have made the production and reflection all the more critical, precise, and calibrated. My thanks go to the Dean of the School of Design and Environment Heng Chye Keng, and the Head of the Department of Architecture Wong Yunn Chii. My appreciation goes to Bobby Wong, Tsuto Sakamoto, Florian Schaetz, Tay Kheng Soon, Khoo Peng Beng and Lai Chee Kien. My gratitude goes to Diane Agrest for her insights into practice, pedagogy, and architecture while I was at the Irwin S. Chanin School of Architecture at the Cooper Union.

To all the patrons who provide for, intervene, and collaborate in so many ways to the design process that more often than not make the work that much better, thank you. I would also like to mention Hanson Ho of H55, whose careful attention to detail and structure has provided a strong and fundamental design framework for this book. And most importantly to my wife who has supported me both intellectually, creatively, and emotionally in more ways than can be counted, this small book is for you.

Project Contributors 2007–2013

Bensko, Heather; Bonifaz, Joaquin;
Cao Zhe Jing; Chan, Juliana;
Chan, Rayanna; Chia, Sean;
Choung Yongsu; Chua Gong Yao;
Conceicao, Stefanie; Ervite, Maria;
Goh, Cassandra; Kuek Chee Ping;
Kwon Seula, Sara;
Lee, Wen Hui Joleen; Leung, Eva;
Liang Yuan Yuan; Lie, Epiphanie;
Lim, Kelvin; Lim Shing Hui;
Loy LiJun; Mei Liang Kai, Alvin;
Nagamalai, Vignesh;
Ng, Ai Lian Sarah; Ng Weiqi;
Ngai, Dixon; Ong, Alistaire;
Oh Pei Yu; Park, Da Song Emily;
Phau, Yun Nong;
Putra, Andrei Seow, Dannie;
Shim Woon-Ok; Tan Bing Hui;
Tan Yuan Zhi; Vltavsky, Grit;
Wong Shujun; Wong, Amanda;
Xiao Ma; Vignesh Nagamalai;
Zapanta, Rommel.

The Venice Biennale (A Ventilated
Display) was designed along with
Khoo Peng Beng, Belinda Huang
and Florian Schaetz.

Project Consultants

Architects of Record
Singapore: HK Hia & Associates,
Stereoscopic House; AKDA
Architects, Hut House; Arya
Architects, A Simple Factory
Building.

Malaysia: DC Akitek (M) & Rakan
Rakan, Pile Houses.

Consultants
TEP Consultants Pte Ltd; DMS
Consulting Engineers; PQS
Consultants; HS Engineering
Consultants; K L Au Consultants;
Jurukur Ecem; Kong & Associates
Consultuans Sdn BHD; Jurutera
JRK Sdn. Bhd Civil & Structural
Engineers; KKC Consultancy
Services; Goh Yong Ping
Mechanical Engineer.

Project
Photo Credits

Amir Sultan
www.livingpod.com
> *pp 182-185, 190, 191, 198, 199;*

Daniel Sheriff
www.danielsheriff.com
> *pp 80, 81, 86, 87, 88 tip-in, 89 tip-in, 95, 98, 99, 108 (top-left and bottom-right image), 109;*

Jing Quek
www.wearesuper.sg
> *pp 204, 207, 210, 212, 213, 216, 216 tip-in, 217, 217 tip-in;*

Kenneth Choo
www.kennethchoo.com
> *pp 222-225, 232, 232 tip-in, 233 tip-in, 233, 234, 235;*

Owen Lam
> *pp 211, 296-299;*

Sanjay Kewlani
www.skewedeye.com
> *pp 264, 265, 274, 275, 279, 280 tip-in, 281 tip-in, 284 (bottom image), 285, 288, 288 tip-in, 289, 289 tip-in;*

Sean Chia
> *pp 122-125, 128 tip-in, 129 tip-in, 130, 131, 133, 134, 136, 137, 160-165, 168, 168 tip-in, 169, 169 tip-in, 172, 176, 177;*

All other photographs by author.

Grit Vltavsky

Lives and works in New York City

Grit Vltavsky, Dipl. Ing., is an architect with considerable design experience in both the residential and public arenas. She has designed spaces at Robert Wilson's Watermill Center, Long Island and the Observatory Park Astronomy Museum, Great Falls, Virginia. She restored the historic building envelope of Unified Science Center, Martin Hall, at the School of Fine Arts, Swarthmore College in Pennsylvania. She has collaborated on many international projects, including the Kennedy Business Center in Eindhoven, Netherlands and the award winning Baumschulenweg crematorium and commemorative hall in Berlin, Germany.

She recently joined RAA as a project manager for the exhibit design of the Museum of Human Rights, under construction in Winnipeg, Canada. Concurrently she runs her own architecture office, researching and designing independent projects. Her interests lie in sustainable materials, meticulous detailing and refined construction. She thoughtfully writes about contemporary design and is active in a range of professional networks.

Grit is also an experienced educator having taught at the School of Architecture at Pratt Institute in New York City and Princeton University, USA where she helped to develop teaching curricula, lecture series and faculty exhibitions. She holds a Masters of Architecture from Princeton University and a Bachelors of Architecture from Cooper Union, where she received the Henry Adams Certificate of Merit. In her native country she earned a diploma in architecture from Universität der Künste and Technische Universität, Berlin. She is a licensed and registered architect in Germany.

Nasrine Seraji

Lives and works in Paris

Erwin Viray

Lives and works in Kyoto

Nasrine Seraji founded Atelier Seraji Architectes & Associés in 1990. Formed by her early experience at London's Architectural Association, she subsequently worked in large architectural offices in England and the United States before coming to France. She is the Dean for the École Nationale Supérieure d'Architecture (ENSA) Paris - Malaquais. She previously directed the Institute of Art and Architecture at the Academy of Fine Arts in Vienna and was professor and chair for architecture at the College of Architecture, Art, and Planning at Cornell University. Seraji has lectured and exhibited widely in Europe, the United States, and Asia.

In addition to having written numerous essays and catalogues on architecture and urbanism, she has been awarded the Médaille d'Argent de la Formation by the French Academy of Architecture, and named Chevalier de l'Ordre des Arts et des Lettres and Chevalier de l'Ordre National du Mérite in France.

Erwin Viray, is a Professor and Head of the Graduate School of Architecture Design at Kyoto Institute of Technology, Award Ambassador for the Holcim Awards, Chairman of the Jury for the Singapore President's Design Awards 2013, Board Member of the TOTO Gallery Ma, and Editor of a+u (Architecture and Urbanism).

Erik L'Heureux

Born in USA in 1973
Lives and works in Singapore

Erik L'Heureux, AIA, LEED AP BD+C is an American architect and educator. He is an Assistant Professor at the National University of Singapore where he does research on tropical envelopes and the architecture of the regions. A former boat builder, he practiced architecture in New York City while teaching at the Irwin S. Chanin School of Architecture at the Cooper Union.

Erik studied architecture at Princeton University from 1997–2000 with Elizabeth Diller and Mario Gandelsonas. He received his Master of Architecture degree in 2000 as a recipient of the Susan K. Underwood Design Award. He also studied architecture as a James W. Fitzgibbon Scholar at Washington University in St Louis from 1992–1996 where he received his Bachelor of Arts in Architecture. He was later honored with a Distinguished Alumni Award in 2006.

Erik is a registered architect in the USA, American Institute of Architects Member, NCARB certified, and a LEED accredited professional. He has won several design awards including a 2013 WAF Design Award, a 2013 FuturArc Green Leadership Architecture Merit Award, a 2012 AIA New York City Design Merit Award, a 2011 President's Design Award from Singapore, and two AIA New York State Design Awards in 2009 and 2007 respectively.

In 2010 Erik was a curator and designer for the Singapore Pavilion at the Architecture Venice Biennale. In 2011 and 2012, Erik co-organized an international overseas program between Washington University in St Louis, the National University of Singapore, and Tongji University for comparative research on the cities of Hong Kong, Shanghai, and Singapore. His design and research work has been published internationally and he lectures widely.

He is married to Joa Kim, a perfumer, and lives together in Singapore with their daughter.

Education

Princeton University,
  Princeton, New Jersey
  Master of Architecture,
  School of Architecture

Washington University,
  St. Louis, Missouri
  Bachelor of Arts
  in Architecture,
  Summa Cum Laude,
  School of Architecture

Professional Accreditations

Registered Architect,
  New York State, USA

Registered Architect,
  State of Rhode Island, USA

AIA
  American Institute
  of Architects, Member

LEED
  Accredited Professional,
  Building Design
  and Construction Specialty

NCARB
  Certified Member #93612

Academic Positions

Assistant Professor, *2008–current*
Lecturer, *2007–2008, 2004*
Visiting Fellow, *2003*
    Department of Architecture
    School of Design and Environment
    National University of Singapore

Associated Faculty
    Lecturer Abroad, Global Urbanism Studio
    Shanghai, Hong Kong, *2011–2012*
    Washington University in St. Louis

Co-Curator and Designer
    Singapore Pavillion Venice Biennale, *2010*

Assistant Professor, Adjunct, *2005*
Instructor, Adjunct, *2001–2003*
    The Cooper Union,
    Irwin S. Chanin School of Architecture

Biographical Notes

1973–1992

Born in Jamestown
Rhode Island, September 21

Lives in Jamestwon
until age 18

Attended high school
in North Kingstown
Rhode Island

Worked as boat builder
& lobsterman, avid sailor

1992–1996

Studied architecture
at the School of Architecture,
Washington University
as a Fitzgibbon Scholar

Worked as a carpenter

Studied drawing and
welding at Rhode Island
School of Design

Received Bachelor of Arts,
Major in Architecture,
Summa Cum Laude

1997–2000

Studied Architecture
at the School of Architecture,
Princeton University

Graduated with
Master of Architecture,
Susan K Underwood
Thesis Prize

Worked in the office
of Agrest+Gandelsonas
Architects, New York City

2000–2003

Taught Architecture
at the Irwin S. Chanin School
of Architecture at the
Cooper Union,
New York City

Worked in various
New York City
Architecture Offices

Guest Critic at Harvard
University, Yale University,
Pratt, New York Institute
of Technology

2003–2004

Moves to Singapore

Visiting Fellow and Lecturer
at the National University of
Singapore

2005–2006

Returns to New York City

Assistant Professor Adjunct
at the Irwin S. Chanin
School of Architecture at
the Cooper Union

Becomes a registered Architect
in New York State,
State of Rhode Island

Guest Critic Cooper Union,
Harvard University

2007

Returns to Singapore

AIA New York State Merit
Design Award

Distinguished Alumni Award,
Washington University
in St. Louis

Lectures at Washington
University in St. Louis, Jury

2008

Conducts International Studio
in Dubai

Publishes Additions
+ Subtractions

AIA New York State Merit
Design Award

Assistant Professor,
Department of Architecture,
National University of
Singapore

2010

Co-Curator and Designer,
Singapore Pavillion
Venice Biennale

Conducts International Studio
in Seim Reap, Cambodia

Lectures at the Venice
Biennal, Archifest Singapore

Publishes Singapore
Transcripts, Probing
Hydrological Urbanism

2011

President's Design Award,
Singapore: 1000 Singapores

Conducts International Studio
in Shanghai with

Washington University, NUS,
and Tongji University

2012

AIA New York Merit
Design Award

Conducts International Studio
in Hong Kong with
Washington Universtiy, NUS

Member of the Singapore
Institute of Landscape
Awards Jury

Exhibits work at the
Center for Architecture,
New York

Lectures at the Academy
of Architecture, Amsterdam,
Urban Research Authority,
Fukuoka, Japan;
Future Cities Laboratory,
ETH Zurich/Singapore;
Urban Redevelopment
Authority Singapore,
Singapore; IfOU
International Conference

2013

FuturArc Green Leadership
Citation Award

CAADRIA Conference 2013

Publishes Singles & Multiples,
Singapore Metropolitan
Region

WAF
Category Winner 2013,
Production/Energy/
Recycling